Infinitely Demanding

8

Infinitely Demanding

Ethics of commitment, politics of resistance

SIMON CRITCHLEY

VERSO

London • New York

First published by Verso 2007
© Simon Critchley 2007
All rights reserved

The moral right of the author has been asserted

1 3 5 7 9 10 8 6 4 2

Verso
UK: 6 Meard Street, London W1F 0EG
USA: 180 Varick Street, New York, NY 10014-4606
www.versobooks.com

Verso is the imprint of New Left Books

ISBN-13: 978-1-84467-121-2

British Library Cataloguing in Publication Data
A catalogue record for this book is available from the British Library

Library of Congress Cataloging-in-Publication Data
A catalog record for this book is available from the Library of Congress

Typeset in Baskerville by Hewer Text UK Ltd, Edinburgh
Printed and bound in Germany by GGP Media GmbH

For my mother, Sheila Patricia Critchley

Contents

Introduction
The possibility of commitment

Philosophy does not begin in an experience of wonder, as ancient tradition contends, but rather, I think, with the indeterminate but palpable sense that something desired has not been fulfilled, that a fantastic effort has failed. Philosophy begins in disappointment. Although there might well be precursors, I see this as a specifically modern conception of philosophy. To give it a name and a date, one could say that it is a conception of philosophy that follows from Kant's Copernican turn at the end of the eighteenth century. The great metaphysical dream of the soul moving frictionless towards knowledge of itself, things-in-themselves and God is just that, a dream. Absolute knowledge or a direct ontology of things as they are is decisively beyond the ken of fallible, finite creatures like us. Human beings are exceedingly limited creatures, a mere vapour or virus can destroy us. The Kantian revolution in philosophy is a lesson in limitation. As Pascal said, we are the weakest reed in nature and this fact requires an acknowledgement that is very reluctantly given. Our culture is endlessly beset with Promethean myths of the overcoming of the human condition, whether through the fantasy of artificial intelligence, contemporary delusions about robotics, cloning and genetic manipulation or simply through cryogenics and cosmetic surgery. We seem to have enormous difficulty in accepting our limitedness, our finiteness, and this failure is a cause of much tragedy.

One could give an entire taxonomy of disappointment, but the two forms that concern me most urgently are religious and political. These forms of disappointment are not entirely separable and continually leak into one another. Indeed, we will see how ethical and religious categories are rightly difficult to distinguish at times, and in my discussions of ethics I will often have recourse to religious traditions. In religious disappointment, that which is desired but lacking is an experience of faith. That is, faith in some transcendent god, god-equivalent or, indeed, gods. Philosophy in the experience of religious disappointment is godless, but it is an uneasy godlessness with a religious memory and within a religious archive.

The experience of religious disappointment provokes the following, potentially abyssal question: if the legitimating theological structures and religious belief systems in which people like us believed are no longer believable, if, to coin a phrase, God is dead, then what becomes of the question of the meaning of life? It is this question that provokes the visit of what Nietzsche refers to as the uncanniest of guests: *nihilism*. Nihilism is the breakdown of the order of meaning, where all that we previously imagined as a divine, transcendent basis for moral valuation has become meaningless. Nihilism *is* this declaration of meaninglessness, a sense of indifference, directionlessness or, at its worst, despair that can flood into all areas of life. For some, this is the defining experience of youth – witness the deaths of numerous young romantics, whether Keats, Shelley, Sid Vicious or Kurt Cobain, and their numbers continue to multiply – for others it lasts a whole lifetime. The philosophical task set by Nietzsche and followed by many others in the Continental tradition is how to respond to nihilism, or better, how to *resist* nihilism. Philosophical activity, by which I mean the free movement of thought and critical reflection, is defined by militant resistance to nihilism. That is, philosophy is defined by the thinking through of the fact that the basis of meaning has become meaningless. Our devalued values require what Nietzsche calls revaluation or trans-valuation. All the difficulty here consists in thinking through the question of meaning without bewitching ourselves with new and exotic forms of meaning, with imported brands of existential balm, the sort of thing that Nietzsche called 'European Buddhism' – although there is a lot 'American Buddhism' around too.

However, this book will be concerned with the other major form of disappointment, political disappointment. In the latter, the sense of something lacking or failing arises from the realization that we inhabit a violently *unjust* world, a world defined by the horror of war, a world where, as Dostoevsky says, blood is being spilt in the merriest way, as if it were champagne. Such an experience of disappointment is acutely tangible at the present time, with the corrosion of established political structures and an unending war on terror where the moods of Western populations are controlled through a politics of fear managed by the constant threat of external attack. As I try to show in the Appendix to this book, this situation is far from novel and might be said to be definitional of politics from antiquity to early and considerably later modernity. My point is that if the present time is defined by a state of war, then this experience of political disappointment provokes the question of justice: what might justice be in a violently unjust world? It is this question that provokes the need for an ethics or what others might call normative principles that might enable us to face and face down the present political situation. The main task of this book is responding to that need by offering a theory of ethical experience and subjectivity that will lead to an infinitely demanding ethics of commitment and politics of resistance (See Figure 1).

Nihilism – active and passive

Yet, the latter is not the only option offered up by the present situation. This is why I mentioned religious disappointment and

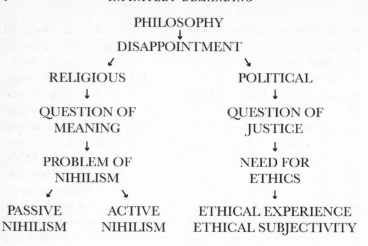

Figure 1

the problem of nihilism. Keeping that problem in mind, the present situation can provoke coherent, but in my view misguided, responses that we might describe as 'passive nihilism' and 'active nihilism'. The passive nihilist looks at the world from a certain distance, and finds it meaningless. He is scornful of the pretensions of liberal humanism with its metaphysical faith in progress, improvement and the perfectibility of humankind, beliefs that he claims are held with the same dogmatic assurance that Christianity was held in Europe until the late eighteenth century. The passive nihilist concludes that we are simply animals, and rather nasty aggressive primates at that, what we might call *homo rapiens*, *rapacious animals*. Rather than acting in the world and trying to transform it, the passive nihilist simply focuses on himself and his particular pleasures and projects for perfecting himself, whether through discovering the inner child, manipulating pyramids, writing pessimistic-sounding literary essays, taking up yoga, bird-watching or botany, as was the case with the aged Rousseau. In the face of the increasing brutality of reality, the passive nihilist tries to achieve a mystical stillness, calm contemplation: 'European Buddhism'. In a world that is all too rapidly blowing itself to pieces, the passive nihilist closes his eyes and makes himself into an island.[1]

The active nihilist also finds everything meaningless, but instead of sitting back and contemplating, he tries to destroy this world and bring another into being. The history of active nihilism is fascinating and a consideration of it would take us back into various utopian, radical political and even terrorist groups. We might begin this history with Charles Fourier's utopian *phalansteries* of free love and leisure, before moving on to late nineteenth-century anarchism in Russia and elsewhere, through to the Promethean activism of Lenin's Bolshevism, Marinetti's Futurism, Maoism, Debord's Situationism, the Red Army Fraction in Germany, the Red Brigades in Italy, the Angry Brigade in England, the Weather Underground in the USA, without forgetting the sweet naivety of the Symbionese Liberation Army.

At the present time, however, the quintessence of active nihilism is al-Qaeda, this covert and utterly postmodern, rhizomatic quasi-corporation outside of any state control. Al-Qaeda uses the technological resources of capitalist globalization – elaborate and coded forms of communication, the speed and fluidity of financial transactions, and obviously transportation – against that globalization. The explicit aim of the destruction of the World Trade Center was the initiation of a new series of religious wars. The sad truth is that this aim has been hugely successful. The legitimating logic of al-Qaeda is that the modern world, the world of capitalism, liberal democracy and secular humanism, is meaningless and that the only way to remake meaning is through acts of spectacular destruction, acts which it is no exaggeration to say have redefined the contemporary political situation and made the pre-9/11 world seem remote and oddly quaint. We are living through a chronic re-theologization of politics.

In my view, one should approach al-Qaeda with the words and actions of bin Laden resonating against those of Lenin, Blanqui,

Mao, Baader-Meinhof, and Durruti. The more one learns about figures like Sayyid Qutb, who was murdered by the Nasser government in Egypt in 1966 after a period of imprisonment when he wrote many texts that would influence intellectuals like al-Zawahiri, Osama bin Laden's mentor, the more one sees the connection between Jihadist revolutionary Islam and more classical forms of extreme revolutionary vanguardism.[2] Although bin Laden's language is always couched in terms of opposing the 'Zionist–Crusader chain of evil' and 'global unbelief', the political logic of Jihadism is an active nihilist revolutionary vanguardism which is far more deeply committed to martyrdom and the rewards of the hereafter than the establishment of any positive social programme. In the savage intensity of his piety, Osama bin Laden is a quasi-kissing cousin of Turgenev's Bazarov.[3]

Motivational deficit

Although they are opposed, both active and passive nihilism are Siamese twins of sorts, as they both agree on the meaninglessness of reality, or rather its essential unreality, which inspires either passive withdrawal or violent destruction. I will be following a different path. It seems to me that that we have to think through and think out of the situation in which we find ourselves. We have to resist and reject the temptation of nihilism and face up to the hard reality of the world. What does that reality teach us? It shows violent injustice here and around the world; it shows growing social and economic inequalities here and around the world; it shows that the difference between what goes on here and around the world is increasingly fatuous. It shows the populations of the well-fed West governed by fear of outsiders, whose current names are 'terrorist', 'immigrant', 'refugee' or 'asylum seeker'. It shows populations turning inward towards some reactionary and xenophobic conception of their purported identity, something which is happening in a particularly frightening manner all across Europe at present. It shows that because of an excessive diet of sleaze, deception, complacency and corruption liberal democracy is not in the best of health. It shows, in my parlance, massive political disappointment.

It is here that we have to recognize the force of al-Qaeda's position and their diagnosis of the present. In a word, the institutions of secular liberal democracy simply do not sufficiently motivate their citizenry. On the contrary, at this point in time, the political institutions of the Western democracies appear strangely demotivating. There is increasing talk of a democratic deficit, a feeling of the irrelevance of traditional electoral politics to the lives of citizens, and an uncoupling of civil society from the state, at the same time as the state seeks to extend ever-increasing powers of surveillance and control into all areas of civil society. I think it might be claimed that there is a motivational deficit at the heart of liberal democratic life, where citizens experience the governmental norms that rule contemporary society as externally binding but not internally compelling.[4] They are simply not part of our mindset, the dispositions of our subjectivity. If secular liberal democracy doesn't motivate subjects sufficiently, then – returning to active and passive nihilism – what seems to motivate subjects are frameworks of belief that call that secular project into question. Whatever one may think about it, one has to recognize that there is something powerfully motivating about the Islamist or Jihadist worldview, or indeed its Christian fundamentalist obverse. Yet, the source of that motivation is metaphysical or theological. What is most depressing about the many depressing features of the current US administration is the sort of metaphysical or theological symmetry between George W. Bush and Osama bin Laden. This is what I mean when I say that we have entered a period of new religious war.

The hypothesis here is that there is a motivational deficit at the heart of secular liberal democracy and that what unites active and passive nihilists is a metaphysical or theological critique of secular democracy, whether in terms of a Jihadist or Christian fundamentalist activism or a Buddhistic passivity. Now, crucially, this motivational deficit is also a *moral* deficit, a lack at the heart of democratic life that is intimately bound up with the felt inadequacy of official secular conceptions of morality. Indeed, following Jay Bernstein here, one might go further and argue that modernity itself has had the effect of generating a motivational deficit in morality that undermines the possibility of ethical secularism.[5] I am not so sure I want to nail my colours to the mast of a defence of secularism, but it brings me to the premise behind the opening chapters of this book. What is required, in my view, is a conception of ethics that begins by accepting the motivational deficit in the institutions of liberal democracy, but without embracing either passive or active nihilism, although each of these positions represents a potent temptation: the sense that the world is irreparably flawed in a way that behoves either passive withdrawal or active destruction. What is lacking at the present time of massive political disappointment is a motivating, empowering conception of ethics that can face and face down the drift of the present, an ethics that is able to respond to and resist the political situation in which we find ourselves. This brings me to my initial question: if we are going to stand a chance of constructing an ethics that empowers subjects to political action, a motivating ethics, we require some sort of answer to what I see as the basic question of morality. It is to this that I would now like to turn.

The argument

How does a self bind itself to whatever it determines as its good? In my view, this is the fundamental question of ethics. To answer it we require a description and explanation of the subjective commitment to ethical action. My claim will be that all questions of normative justification, whether with reference to theories of justice, rights, duties, obligations or whatever, should be referred to what I call 'ethical experience'. Ethical experience elicits the core structure of moral selfhood, what we might think of as the existential matrix of ethics. As such, and this is what really interests me, ethical experience furnishes an account of the motivational force to act morally, of that by virtue of which a self decides to pledge itself to some conception of the good. My polemical contention is that without a plausible account of motivational force, that is, without a conception of the ethical subject, moral reflection is reduced to the empty manipulation of the standard justificatory frameworks: deontology, utilitarianism and virtue ethics.

The initial task of Chapter 1 is twofold: first, to outline a theory of ethical experience based on the concepts of approval and demand; and second, to show how this theory presupposes a model of ethical subjectivity. I then go on to explore this notion of ethical experience with particular attention to Kant's notion of practical reason and how that notion is picked up and adapted in an influential way by contemporary Kantians, such as Rawls, Korsgaard and Habermas. The central focus of the discussion of Kant will be the peculiar doctrine of the 'fact of reason' which attempts to unify the justification of moral norms on the basis of universality with the motivation to act on those norms.

My overall argument can be broken down into meta-ethical and normative parts. I understand meta-ethics to be inquiry into the nature of ethics and what makes ethics the thing that it is, i.e. what makes ethics ethical; I understand normative ethics to be the recommendation of a specific conception of morality. On the basis of my meta-ethical argument about ethical experience in Chapter 1 and illustrated with the example of Kant, I will go in on in Chapters 2 and 3 to construct a normative model of ethical subjectivity. I will recommend this model most warmly, although I don't think it is the business of moral argument to be able to provide watertight proofs for its propositions. Ethical argument is neither like logic, which is deductively true, nor science, which is inductively true. There is a point at which the rationality of moral argumentation gives way to moral recommendation, even exhortation, an appeal to the individual reader from an individual writer.

The central philosophical task in my approach to ethics is developing a theory of ethical subjectivity. A subject is the name for the way in which a self binds itself to some conception of the good and shapes its subjectivity in relation to that good. To be clear, I am not making the questionable claim that it is the job of philosophers to manufacture moral selves. They exist already as the living, breathing products of education and socialization. What I am seeking to offer is a model of ethical subjectivity with some normative force that might both describe and deepen the activity of those living, breathing moral selves. I construct a model of ethical subjectivity by borrowing three concepts from three thinkers. From Alain Badiou, I borrow the idea of *fidelity* to the event as the central ethical experience, which I link to the neglected and much-maligned concept of commitment. From the little-known Danish theologian Knud Ejler Løgstrup, I take the idea of the ethical demand, which is a one-sided, radical and – crucially, for me – *unfulfillable* demand. From Emmanuel Levinas, I take the idea that the unfulfillability of the ethical demand, what he sometimes calls 'the curvature of intersubjective space', is internal to subjectivity. The thought here is that the Levinasian ethical subject is a subject defined by the experience of an internalized demand that it can never meet, a demand that exceeds it, what he calls infinite responsibility. For Levinas, the experience of the demand is affective and the affect that constitutes the ethical subject is trauma. Following this clue, I seek to reconstruct the basic operation of Levinas's work in psychoanalytic terms, borrowing the notion of trauma in the later Freud. This means that the ethical subject is, in my parlance, *hetero-affectively* constituted. It is a *split subject* divided between itself and a demand that it cannot meet, a demand that makes it the subject that it is, but which it cannot entirely fulfill. The sovereignty of my autonomy is always usurped by the heteronomous experience of the other's demand. The ethical subject is a *dividual*.

In Chapter 3, I show how this conception of the ethical subject runs the risk of chronically overloading – indeed masochistically persecuting – the self with responsibility in a way that calls for an experience of what psychoanalysts call sublimation. Drawing heavily from Lacan, the problem of sublimation will take us into psychoanalytic discussions of art and, more specifically, tragedy. I argue that the psychoanalytic discourse on sublimation is hostage to a 'tragic-heroic paradigm' that extends back through Heidegger to German Idealism. Against this paradigm, I will show how *humour* can be conceived as a practice of minimal sublimation that both maintains and alleviates the division of the ethical subject.

So, on my view, the ethical subject is defined by commitment or fidelity to an unfulfillable demand, a demand that is internalized subjectively and which divides subjectivity. Now, such a divided subjectivity is, I would argue, the experience of *conscience*, which is a concept that I want to place back at the heart of ethics. Despite Nietzschean claims about conscience culminating in self-hatred or Freudian claims about the cruelty of the super-ego, I am proposing an ethics of discomfort, a hyperbolic ethics based on the internalization of an unfulfillable ethical demand. Such a conscience is not, as Luther puts it, the work of God in the heart of man, but rather the work of ourselves upon ourselves. Such formulations bring Foucault's late work to mind. But I do not understand this work of the self upon itself in Foucault's sense, which always seems to be orientated around practices of self-mastery, what he calls 'care for the self as a practice of freedom'.[6] On the contrary, for me, the experience of conscience is that of an essentially divided self, an originally inauthentic humorous self that can never attain the autarchy of self-mastery.

The question then becomes, and this is the theme of the final

chapter: what is the link between conscience and political action? I
pursue this through a reading of Marx, particularly the early Marx
and more particularly still the figure of what he calls 'true
democracy' in his early critique of Hegel. I see this figure as a
clue for a thinking of the political in Marx's work against the
tendency towards economistic reductionism that was emphasized
by Engels and became an article of faith for the Marxism of the
Second International. My use of Marx is not scholarly or philological, but diagnostic. I am interested in his work because some of
his analyses and concepts tell us a good deal about who we are,
where we are, and how we might change who and where we are.
This chapter turns around, to coin a phrase, what is living and
what is dead in Marx's work. On the one hand, I defend Marx's
diagnosis of capitalism and argue that his socio-economic insights
have become more plausible in the face of what we all too glibly
call globalization. Yet, on the other hand, I criticize the belief that
the development of capitalism leads ineluctably to the simplification of the class structure into the opposed poles of bourgeoisie and
proletariat, where the latter becomes the political subject of
revolutionary communist praxis. Yet, if the proletariat is no longer
the revolutionary subject, then this raises a deep question as to the
nature of political subjectivity. After a discussion of the formation
of political subjectivity that draws on Gramsci's concept of hegemony and Ernesto Laclau's recovery and elaboration of that
concept, I go on to consider the possibility of political organization
at the present time. In particular, I consider the meaning that can
be given to figures like association and coalition in the face of the
radical dislocations of global capitalism. I discuss the politics of
indigenous identity as a powerful example of the invention of a new
political subject, before moving on to the spectacular tactical
politics of contemporary anarchism, which I think has forged a
new language of civil disobedience.

Circling back to the main argument of the book, I conclude by
arguing that at the heart of a radical politics there has to be what I

call a *meta-political* ethical moment that provides the motivational force or propulsion into political action. If ethics without politics is empty, then politics without ethics is blind. Taking my cue from a heterodox reading of Levinas, I claim that this meta-political moment is *anarchic,* where ethics is the disturbance of the political status quo. Ethics is anarchic meta-politics, it is the continual questioning from below of any attempt to impose order from above. On this view, politics is the creation of *interstitial distance* within the state, the invention of new political subjectivities. Politics, I argue, cannot be confined to the activity of government that maintains order, pacification and security while constantly aiming at consensus. On the contrary, politics is the manifestation of dissensus, the cultivation of an anarchic multiplicity that calls into question the authority and legitimacy of the state. It is in relation to such a multiplicity that we may begin to restore some dignity to the dreadfully devalued discourse of democracy.

1

Demanding approval – a theory of ethical experience

Ethical Experience

What do I mean by ethical experience? I would like to begin by trying to pick out the formal structure of ethical experience, or what, with Dieter Henrich, we can call the grammar of the concept of moral insight.[1] Firstly, with the word 'experience' in the ethical domain I do not mean a passive display of externally received images in the theatre of consciousness. Experience is not sheer passivity. Rather, ethical experience is an *activity* whereby new objects emerge for a subject involved in the process of their creation. This distinction between passive and active experience broadly follows that between *Erlebnis* and *Erfahrung* in Hegel, where the latter suggests the ongoing, processual character of experience. Ethical experience is activity, the activity of the subject, even when that activity is the receptivity to the other's claim upon me – it is an active receptivity.

In my view, ethical experience begins with the experience of a demand to which I give my approval. There are two key components to ethical experience: *approval* and *demand* (See Figure 2). Let me begin by unpacking the notion of approval. I claim that there can be no sense of the good – however that is filled out at the level of content, and I understand it for the moment in an entirely formal and empty manner – without an act of approval, affirmation or

THE STRUCTURE OF ETHICAL EXPERIENCE

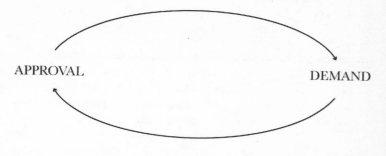

Figure 2

approbation. That is, the ethical statement 'love thy neighbour as thyself' differs from the epistemic claim that 'I am now seated in a chair'. Why? Because my ethical statement implies an *approval* of the activity of loving one's neighbour, whereas I can be quite indifferent to the chair I am sitting on. If I say, to use a less common moral example, that 'it would be good for parrots to receive the right to vote in elections', then my saying this implies that I approve of this development.

However, this is not to say that approval is absent from epistemic claims or factual statements. One might legitimately object that if I say 'there is a large portion of baltic herring on the table', then my saying this implies a tacit approval of that fact, for I am particularly partial to the aforementioned herring. Alternatively, if I say 'there is a dead rat in my fridge', or, with Peter Sellars's Inspector Clouseau that, 'there is a bomb in my room', then my factual statements imply strong disapproval, a disapproval, moreover, bordering on the moral assertion that it is not good for me to have a rat in my fridge or a bomb in my room. On this view, the difference between factual and moral statements with respect to approval is a difference of degree and not a difference of kind. My point is simply that there *is* a difference of degree and that moral statements imply strong approval or disapproval of the states of affairs under discussion, e.g. 'war is always wrong!' or 'evil must not be appeased but attacked!'; 'abortion is murder!' or 'every woman should have the right to choose!'; 'Famine relief is essential!' or 'charity begins at home!' Both factual and moral statements imply an experience of approval and the difference between them might be said to consist in the *strength* of that approval, ranging from a more or less indifferent assent or neutral acquiescence to an existential affirmation or commitment that leads to action.

However, although the good only comes into view through approval, it is not good *by virtue* of approval. That approval is an approval *of* something, namely a demand that demands approval. In my example, the approval of parrots receiving the right to vote is related to the fact that – at least in my singular moral imagination – parrots make a certain demand, namely the demand for political representation. Ethical experience is, first and foremost, the approval of a demand, a demand that demands approval. As is suggested by Figure 2, ethical experience has to be circular, although hopefully only virtuously so. As Heidegger famously shows against the accusation of the circularity of Cartesian reasoning, not all circles are vicious.

Leaving parrots to one side, and turning to the history of philosophy and religion, we can think about how this formal concept of demand can be filled out with various contents. Here is a list of demands for approval that can be inserted on the right side of Figure 2: Mosaic Law in the Bible, the Good beyond Being in Plato, the resurrected Christ in Paul and Augustine, the Good as the goal of desire for Aquinas, the practical ideal of generosity for Descartes, the experience of benevolence for Hutcheson, and of sympathy for Adam Smith and Hume, the greatest happiness of the greatest number for Bentham and Mill, the moral law in Kant, practical faith as the goal of subjective striving in Fichte, the abyssal intuition of freedom in Schelling, the creature's feeling of absolute dependency on a creator in Schleiermacher, pity for the suffering of one's fellow human beings in Rousseau or for all creatures in Schopenhauer, the thought of eternal return in Nietzsche, the ethico-teleological idea in the Kantian sense for Husserl, the call of conscience in Heidegger, the relation to the Thou in Buber, the claim of the non-identical in Adorno, etc., etc. This list might be extended.

The point is that each of these positions is the expression of a demand to which the self gives its approval, and that this structure of demand and approval gives the shape of ethical experience. The essential feature of ethical experience is that the subject of the demand – the moral self – affirms that demand, assents to finding it good, binds itself to that good and shapes its subjectivity in relation to that good. We will extend this very short history of ethics with the example of Kant and some contemporary Kantians and post-Kantians, but note that my little list has some big gaps, some of which will be discussed presently.

What I called above the virtuous circularity of ethical experience raises the following question: which comes first, demand or approval? *Prima facie,* one is perhaps inclined to say that the demand comes first; that is, without some sort of demand there is nothing to approve. This would appear to be true experientially. Let me take two examples: (i) Bob Geldof, London-based Irish rockstar turned activist and philanthropist, and (ii) the resurrection of Christ. In late autumn 1984, Bob Geldof experienced the demand of Ethiopian famine victims during an enormously distressing BBC newscast. Approving of this demand, he became subjectively committed to doing something to alleviate their plight, and thus the Band-Aid and Live-Aid projects were born. Much money was raised, much good was done, and Bob eventually became Sir Bob. Indeed, an even more dreadful version of the Band-Aid single was released late in 2004 and outsold all other songs on the UK Christmas market, and the twentieth anniversary of Live-Aid was marked with 'Make Poverty History' concerts in July 2005 which were rather neatly coopted by the vapid universalism of Blair's New Labour. QED for the priority of demand over approval, it would seem. However, another person watching the same newscast as Sir Bob in 1984 might have experienced no demand at all. Or indeed, in the case of the immoralist whom we shall meet in a moment, they might have approved of the demand, but nonetheless done nothing about it.

If this seems to be an argument from moral callousness, then consider another example, that of Christ's resurrection. To the believer, the resurrection is a fact, a fact which places a demand upon the self, and it is in relation to that demand that Christian subjectivity takes shape. Yet, to the non-believer there is just an empty tomb, the grave of the troublesome radical rabbi Jesus executed by the occupying Roman authorities with the connivance of the Pharisees. The point is that the demand is not somehow objectively given in the state of affairs. Rather, the demand is only felt *as* a demand for the self who approves of it. Therefore, although experientially (in the life of the believer or Sir Bob) it is as if the demand precedes the approval of the demand, one is obliged to conclude that demand and approval arise at the same time and that the demand is only felt as a demand by a subject who approves of it. Hence, once again, the circularity of ethical experience.

Yet, one might object to this picture of ethical experience in the following terms: if moral statements are, on my account, characterized by strong approval or disapproval of a state of affairs, then how can one deal with the fact that such statements can be made ironically or sarcastically? It is admittedly incontestable that the words 'love thy neighbour as thyself' can be uttered with a sneer rather than be sincere. But this simply shows that the statement is being made without strong approval or affirmation, where its implications for action are held at a safe ironic distance rather than becoming internal to the dispositions of moral self-hood. It is a case of excessively weak approval. But this opens onto a more far-reaching objection, that of the immoralist who might approve of statements such as 'make poverty history' or 'famine relief is essential', but do nothing about them. When the famine relief volunteer knocks at the front door, the immoralist refuses to get off his sofa. In this case, a moral statement might be acknowledged to be legitimate, but is rejected as a maxim for action; the ethical demand is recognized as a demand, but its approval does not entail that one does anything about it. In an important sense, there can be no knock-down response to this objection because the immoralist, like the ironist, can always slip away from making any commitments that would lead from the approval of a demand to action based on that approval. My point is twofold: first that the model of ethical experience provides a way of approaching morality in terms of an affirmation or approved demand that hopefully elicits what I called above the existential matrix of ethics. Second, ethical experience furnishes a possible acount of the motivational force to act morally, of the way in which a conception of the good *can* move the will to act. This does not imply that an approved demand, say in the case of the immoralist, *must* move the will to act. Indeed if it did make that implication, then it would be self-defeating as it would eliminate the free activity of the self from the moral realm. The possibility of bad faith is and has to be the long shadow cast by moral commitment. One might exhort, cajole or quarrel with the immoralist, but one must not force him or her to act morally.

Ethical subjectivity

It might already be apparent that my claim about ethical experience being constituted in a demand which I approve is also a claim about the nature of the self. Let me try and clarify this concept of selfhood or ethical subjectivity by advancing two theses, one hopefully uncontroversial and the other a little more controversial.

1. The self is something that shapes itself through its relation to whatever it determines as its good, whether that is the Torah, the resurrected Christ, the moral law, the community in which I live, suffering humanity, all God's creatures, or whatever. That is, if the demand of the good requires the approval of that demand in order to be experienced *as* a demand, then that approval is given by a self. Who else could give it? The demand of the good requires the strong approval of the self, otherwise we would be either in the uneasy Rousseauesque dilemma of forcing people to be free, or accepting that moral action consists in the ironic manipulation of norms for which one has no personal commitment – a particularly brutal form of moral externalism. If we turn now to Figure 3, an *ethical subject* can be defined as a self relating itself approvingly, bindingly, to the demand of its good. Ethical experience presupposes the existence of an experiencing subject. Hopefully, that's uncontroversial. It's a simple deduction.

2. Now, more controversially, this claim about the relation of presupposition between ethical experience and the subject of that experience can be deepened in the following way. I have argued that the demand of the good requires approval by a self in order to be experienced as a demand. As such, moral life is an aspect of what it means to be a self, that can be placed alongside other areas of life: epistemic, aesthetic, political and so on. So far, so good. However, one can go on and argue more forcefully that this demand of the good *founds* the self; or, better, that the demand of the good is the fundamental principle of the subject's articulation. What we think of as a self is fundamentally an ethical subject, a self that

ETHICAL SUBJECTIVITY

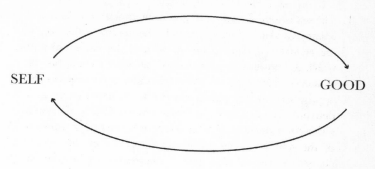

SELF

GOOD

Figure 3

is constituted in a relation to its good, a self – our self – that is organized around certain core values and commitments. Of course, this is another way of claiming the primacy of practical reason to which we will return when we examine Kant.

This second thesis is best argued negatively, through the experience of failure, betrayal and evil. Namely, that if I act in such a way that I know to be evil, then I am acting in a manner destructive of the self that I am, or that I have chosen to be. I have failed myself or betrayed myself. Once again, such a claim is quite formal and does not presuppose any specific content to the good, let alone any moralistic prudishness. For example, my good could be perpetual peace or permanent revolution, merciful meekness or bloody vengeance, the Kantian moral law or the Sadean *droit de jouir*, where the Divine Marquis believed that one's right to have an orgasm with whosoever one chose whenever one felt so inclined required the construction of specifically designated sex houses in the streets of Paris. The point here is that the ethical subject is constituted in relation to a demand that is determined as good, and that this can be felt most acutely when I fail to act in accordance with that demand or when I deliberately transgress it and betray myself. I can be as much a failing Sadist as a failing Kantian.

This is why Plato is perfectly consequent when he claims that vice is destructive of self, the deeper point being that the experience of whatever we determine as vice reveals in a negative profile the self that I have chosen to be. Anyone who has tried – and failed – to cure themselves of some form of addiction, whether cigarettes, alchohol, merciful meekness or Sadism, will understand what is meant here. Let me take an example close to my own heart (or lungs), that of smoking. Let's say that having been a committed smoker for most of my adult life, I decide to quit. I might say to myself repeatedly in the manner of a mantra: 'I am a non-smoker, my conception of the good excludes smoking, which is bad. It killed my father and I won't let it kill me. I promised my mother, my sister and my partner that I would stop.' And yet, I find myself at a party, perhaps in a strange place at the end of a stressful journey, where I am due to give a lecture on a topic that I find particularly difficult. It is a summer's evening, the fresh trout at dinner is exquisite, the local wine is pleasingly robust, the company is new and charming. A few drinks later, I am offered and accept a cigarette and enjoy the transgression immeasurably. The transgression is repeated several times until late in the night. The following morning I wake up with a throbbing head, a sore throat and a mind full of self-loathing. In the shower, I convince myself I can feel a malignant cancerous growth under my left shoulder blade.

What has taken place here is that the ethical subject that I have chosen to be enters into conflict with the self that I am, producing a divided experience of self as self-failure. As will be familiar to many of us, the affect or emotion that accompanies this experience is *guilt*. Guilt is the affect that produces a certain splitting or division in the subject, something that Saint Paul understood rather well, 'For the good that I would I do not: but the evil which I would not, that I do'.[2] This experience of self-division is the genesis of the *morsus conscientiae*, the sting of bad conscience, what Joyce – in Anglo-Irish Middle English – calls '*the agenbite of inwit*'. Nietzsche, who in many ways is the Siamese twin of Saint Paul, calls bad conscience 'This most uncanny and most interesting plant of all our earthly vegetation'.[3] The guilty conscience is a strange fruit, for Nietzsche a late fruit, and we shall return to the question of split ethical subjectivity in some detail below when we turn to that most oddly perfect of Nietzscheans, Emmanuel Levinas.

However, the point at issue here is that the phenomenon of guilty conscience reveals – negatively – the fundamentally moral articulation of the self. Namely, that ethical subjectivity is not just an aspect or dimension of subjective life, it is rather the fundamental feature of what we think of as a self, the repository of our deepest commitments and values. Ethical experience presupposes an ethical subject disposed towards the approved demand of its good.

Justifying reasons and exciting reasons

In my view, all questions of normativity, whether universalistic or relativistic, have to follow from some conception of what I am calling ethical experience. That is, without the experience of a demand to which I am prepared to bind myself, to commit myself, the whole business of morality would either not get started or would be a mere manipulation of empty formulae. At the basis of ethics, there has to be some experience of an approved demand, an existential affirmation that shapes my ethical subjectivity and which is the source of my motivation to act.

In this regard, as a contemporary illustration, consider Axel Honneth's quasi-Humean critique of Habermas's moral rationalism on the point that discourse ethics lacks an adequate account of motivation to moral action because there is a gap between universal pragmatics and everyday experience.[4] Honneth attempts to respond to this lack by supplementing the Habermasian theory of justice with a conception of the good based in an account of recognition (*Anerkennung*). This is the recognition of a demand, in Honneth's case the demand for love as the basic prerequisite for self-realization. The claim here is that it is only on the basis of such a story about recognition that what Habermas calls 'the other of justice', namely solidarity, can be more than an abstraction. Of course, the irony is that Honneth's critique of Habermas replicates precisely the guiding intention of Habermas's early work, namely the attempted unification of knowledge and human interests in a critical and emancipatory concept of reflection that would escape any reductive positivistic explanation. It remains an open question, however, to what extent Habermas's later work succeeds or falls short of this laudable intention.

As is always the case in philosophy, this is really a much older debate that goes back at least to Francis Hutcheson's critique of moral rationalism in the 1720s and his useful distinction between *justifying reasons* that legitimate an action on the grounds of generality or universality, or indeed custom, authority and tradition, and *exciting reasons* that would lead a subject to perform such an action in the first place. For Hutcheson, the springs of morality find their source in the sentiment of benevolence that he believed to be common to all persons. For Hutcheson, and for the tradition of moral sense theory that he inspires, namely Adam Smith and Hume, but also Rousseau and Schopenhauer, there can be no account of exciting reasons, and hence no motivating moral theory, without a theory of moral sentiments, affections or passions.[5] This is the role of sympathy for Smith and Hume, and compassion or pity for Rousseau and Schopenhauer. We shall have occasion to go back to the question of the passions when we turn to psychoanalysis later in this book.

However, the basic problem with Hutcheson, and this is something one finds in Hume's and Kant's critiques of moral sense theory, is the following: whilst the critique of Mandeville's moral egoism is admirable, and the critique of moral rationalism with reference to moral sense, affection or passion might well be justified, what is not justified is the assumption of commonality that Hutcheson assumes for his position. Namely, how can one assume that the feeling of benevolence is universal? More pointedly, why should I approve of Hutcheson's benevolence rather than Mandeville's egotistical self-interest? The commonality of benevolence is simply an assumption, and the argument for its priority over self-interest is sheer assertion.[6] Thus, Hutcheson's account of moral sense lacks universality and risks reducing morality to simple empirical inclination.

This raises the following vast question: can ethics be both generalizable and subjectively felt, both universalizable and rooted in our moral selfhood, or are these two halves of a dialectic that cannot be reconciled? Such is what Michael Smith describes as 'the moral problem', which for him is essentially a problem for philosophers although I believe it points towards something much deeper in the relation between moral theory and moral life.[7] In Smith's terms, beginning from a Humean psychology, there is a contradiction between beliefs and desires, that is, between moral beliefs which can be rationally vindicated, and the desires which motivate action on those beliefs, but which may or may not attach themselves to such beliefs. To return to the example of the immoralist, I may be rationally convinced that giving to famine relief is the right thing to do and yet not give because I am insufficiently motivated due to indifference, distraction or laziness. For Smith, there is a contradiction between the *objectivity* of morality, namely that we want to believe that our moral views are right independent of our subjective inclinations and can be rationally defended, and the *practicability* of morality, where having a moral view is supposed to be linked to what we are motivated to do. If the objectivity and practicability of moral judgement are pulling in opposite directions, if morality is not both generalizable and subjectively felt, then perhaps the very idea of morality is incoherent. Although this is not Smith's concern and certainly not his solution to the moral problem, it is to this threat of incoherence that I believe Kant responds. We will see whether or not it is a coherent response.

Kant, for example – the fact of reason

Kant calls that which would produce the power to act morally, the motivational force that would dispose the self towards the good, 'the philosopher's stone'.[8] However, for Kant, such a story about motivation cannot, as for Hutcheson and the moral sense theorists, resolve itself with reference to the passions or moral sentiments like benevolence, sympathy or compassion because that would reduce morality to inclination, and rationality to what Kant calls 'pathology'. The key question of Kant's critical philosophy insofar as it subscribes to the primacy of practical reason is simply: *how can pure reason be practical?* Kant recognizes that the response to this question requires some sort of account of the connection of reason to interest or motivation, but this cannot be an empirical or pathological interest (particular beliefs, inclinations and desires), but must be what he calls a 'pure interest' or, even more oddly, an 'a priori feeling', namely respect for the moral law.

So how can Kant find the philosopher's stone? The question of ethical experience in Kant resolves itself in the seemingly contradictory notion of *the fact of reason* (*das Faktum der Vernunft*).[9] I say 'seemingly contradictory' for how could reason, which is the faculty of apriori cognitions, take on aposteriori, factual form? How could there be a facticity of reason? Wouldn't that require the sort of intellectual intuition explicitly forbidden by the epistemological strictures of the First Critique? For Kant, the fact of reason is the claim that there is a *Faktum* which places a demand on the subject and to which the subject assents. That is, there is a demand of the good, for Kant the consciousness of the moral law, of which the subject approves, and this demand has an immediate, incontrovertible, even apodictic certainty that is *analogous* to the binding power of an empirical fact or *Tatsache*. The difference between the apodicticity of a *Faktum der Vernunft* and an empirical *Tatsache* is that the demand of the fact of reason is only evident insofar as the subject approves it. Of such an apodictic *Faktum*, Kant insists, no example can be found: 'The moral law is given, as an apodictically certain fact, as it were, of pure reason, a fact of which we are a priori conscious, even if it is granted that *no example could be found* in which it has been followed exactly.'[10] The fact of reason is only experienced as the certainty of demand by the subject who approves of it – virtuous circularity once again.

However things may stand with the doctrine of the fact of reason, Dieter Henrich argues, rightly I think, that the entire rational universality of the categorical imperative and Kantian moral theory follows from this experience of moral insight, or what I am calling 'ethical experience'. The function of the fact of reason in Kant is to try to close the gap between justification and motivation. The philosopher's stone would consist precisely in establishing the link between the motivational power of the fact of reason and the rational universality of the categorical imperative. In this way, reason would be identical with the will to reason and the perennial question, 'why should I be moral?', would be answered.

The auto-authentification of the moral law – some contemporary Kantians

Let me try to unpack this Kantian argument in a little more detail by turning to some contemporary Kantians, in particular John Rawls's compelling reconstruction of the fact of reason in his

Lectures on the History of Moral Philosophy.[11] The ambition of Kant's ethics is twofold: firstly, to show that the moral law has objective validity, that it is binding upon practical reasoning; and secondly, that the moral law applies to *us*, it is something we can act *from* and not merely in accordance *with*. In Michael Smith's terms, Kant is trying to address the moral problem by reconciling objectivity with practicability. To achieve this twofold ambition, Rawls identifies four conditions that must be met by the categorical imperative.

1. *The content condition* – that the categorical imperative must not be formal and empty, but must specify requirements on moral deliberation, i.e. that maxims or norms of action must be shown to be capable of deliberation on the basis of the categorical imperative.
2. *The freedom condition* – that the categorical imperative must represent the moral law as something we freely will, i.e. morality must flow from the principle of autonomy.

However, in order for the moral law to be authoritative for us, such that we act from it and not merely in accordance with it, two further conditions are required.

3. *The fact of reason condition* – that the authority of the moral law must be practically located in our everyday moral thought, feeling and judgement.
4. *The motivation condition* – that the consciousness of the moral law as supremely authoritative for us must be so rooted in our person that this law, by itself, is sufficient motive for us to act.

In order to actualize pure practical reason, all four conditions must be met. Conditions 1 and 2, although absolutely essential, would remain abstract and remote without conditions 3 and 4; that is, we would have moral objectivity without practicability. Condition 4 provides the deep structure of 3, showing how the consiousness of the moral law is so rooted in our ethical subjectivity, regardless of natural desires and animal inclinations, that it is sufficient motive for us to act. Kant's most lyrical moments are those when he describes the manner in which the subject is filled with awe at 'the starry heavens above me and the moral law within me'.[12]

The fact of reason is our consciousness of the moral law as supremely authoritative and regulative for us, as something we act from and not merely in accordance with. If we keep this is mind, then we can see the huge problem that it solves for Kant's critical project. It cannot be that our knowledge of the moral law is based upon a consciousness of freedom because that would require the kind of intellectual intuition forbidden by the argument of the First Critique and reintroduced in diverse ways by Fichte and Schelling. Rather, Kant's position is the reverse: the fact of reason is the basic fact from which our moral conception of ourselves as free must begin. Rawls writes,

> The significance of the fact of reason is that pure practical reason exhibits its reality in this fact and in what this fact discloses, namely our freedom. Once we recognize the fact of reason and its significance, all disputations that question the possibility of pure practical reason are vain. No metaphysical or scientific theories can put it in jeopardy.[13]

This raises the following fascinating question in Kant's ethics: namely, what kind of authentification does the moral law have? Famously, Kant claims that whilst freedom is the *ratio essendi* of the moral law, we can have no intuition of freedom for the reasons set out in the First Critique. Therefore, the moral law is the *ratio cognoscendi* of freedom. However, the only authentification of the moral law as binding upon us is the fact of reason. The latter is the subjective guarantee of the determination of the will by the moral law. Rawls continues,

> In the Second Critique, Kant recognizes . . . and accepts the
> view that pure practical reason, with the moral law (via the
> categorical imperative) as its first principle, is authenticated by
> the fact of reason and in turn by that fact's authenticating, in
> those who accept the moral law as binding . . .[14]

That is to say, the only authentification or justification for the
moral law as binding upon us follows from the fact that there are
subjects who recognize that the moral law has this binding power.
To push this a little further, the fact of reason is the *auto-authentification* or *self-justification* of the moral law. Kant closes the gap
between justification and motivation or objectivity and practicability in ethics by making the fact of reason the self-justifying
motivational force for moral action.

What the problem of the fact of reason shows, I think, is the
fragile necessity at the heart of Kant's ethics, and indeed the entire
critical project insofar as freedom is the 'keystone of the whole
architecture of the system of pure reason'.[15] Morality is rooted in
the self-justifying or auto-authenticating approval of the demand of
the fact of reason, a fact that is not reducible to empirical intuition
and of which *'no example can be found'*. If Kant offered more empirical
or experiential substance to the fact of reason, then he would risk
relativizing it in the way we saw criticized in Hutcheson and we
would have practicability without objectivity. If Kant offered less
subjective appeal to the fact of reason, then he would risk reducing
the moral law to an abstraction and we would have objectivity
without practicability.

This problematic of the fact of reason can be shown to be at
work in other contemporary moral philosophers of Kantian
inspiration. Let me take the examples of Jürgen Habermas, Onora
O'Neill and Christine Korsgaard. In the very final words of his
1972 Postscript to *Knowledge and Human Interests*, Habermas notes
that the ambition of a theory of communicative action would be to
show how transcendental features of reasoning and argumentation

are built into the very praxis of social life. In other words, the formal universality of Kantianism has its feet set in the concrete of Hegelian ethical life. He then makes the following fascinating remark, which we have already anticipated in Honneth's critique discussed above,

> Since empirical speech is only *possible* by virtue of the fundamental norms of rational speech, the cleavage between a real and an inevitably idealized (if only hypothetically ideal) community of language is built not only into the process of argumentative reasoning but into the very life-praxis of social systems. *In this way, perhaps the Kantian notion of the fact of reason can be revitalized.*[16]

In other words, the ambition of Habermas's theory of communicative action is the revitalization of the Kantian notion of the fact of reason where the implicit rationality of discourse would reconcile justification and motivation, objectivity and practicability in morality.

In *Towards Justice and Virtue*, O'Neill recognizes the problem of motivation as a real problem for her post-metaphysical reworking of Kantian ethics. O'Neill redescribes universalizability as *followability*, namely that reasons for action must be reasons for all, but she remains silent on the topic of motivation, although followability must be followable by an ethical subject and hence implicitly motivating.[17] A rather different variation on the Kantian position can be found in Christine Korsgaard's *The Sources of Normativity*.[18] On the one hand, she defends the Kantian view that reflective endorsement is morality itself: namely, that maxims or norms of action have to be subject to critical scrutiny before being either rejected or endorsed. Negatively stated, this means that if maxims cannot be willed as universal laws, then they must not be accepted. This is classically Kantian. However, on the other hand, Korsgaard acknowledges the implicitly Hegelian critique of this

Kantian position, as indeed does Habermas, namely that reflective endorsement is open to the charge that the price of universality in ethics is abstraction and formality, where the Kantian subject – like some latter day Stoic – resolutely wills universal maxims that have no place in actual ethical life. To counter this objection, Korsgaard advances the notion of *practical identity*, which is her attempt to rework and 'thicken' Kant's notion of the Kingdom of Ends: namely, that one's moral action is as a self embedded in personal relationships and the networks of family, community and the like. The notion of practical identity has a distinct family resemblance to the problem that Kant wishes to address in the fact of reason, namely to show how moral motivation takes root in our very person and its willed commitments.[19]

The autonomy orthodoxy and the question of facticity

The basic principle of Kant's ethics is autonomy. That is, the only maxims upon which I should act are ones that I will myself, that I give myself. Thus, I am the only source of moral authority and Kantians are and have to be self-legislators. If this were not the case, then I would not be acting freely, but would be acting on norms that I had not myself chosen. If the source of moral authority lies outside myself, in God, the monarch, my employer, tradition, or any norm or norms which I feel as *externally* binding, then I am acting heteronomously, not autonomously.

However – and this is the basic operation of Kant's ethics – I am a rational being and furthermore all human beings are rational. For Kant, rationality is the principle of humanity, which is what Rawls calls in one florid moment, 'the aristocracy of all'.[20] If human beings are rational beings, then the norms that govern the practical lives of humans must be chosen from reason rather than sentiment, which is always particular and contingent. Therefore, in choosing norms rationally for myself I necessarily choose them for all humanity. In making the law for myself, I am making the law for any human being. Therefore, autonomy in ethics entails universality: the only norms upon which I can legitimately act are those which I can consistently will as a universal law. Such is the argument for the categorical imperative in Kant.

Returning to our earlier argument, we have seen that the fact of reason is our consciousness of the determination of the will by the moral law, and therefore the condition of possibility of morality. Now, because Kant's moral theory is based on the principle of autonomy, the fact of reason has to correspond to the will of the subject. The fact of reason is, indeed, a *fact*. Experientially, it is the *otherness* of a demand. But this demand has to correspond to the subject's autonomy. It is a fact that has to be an *act*. In other words, the ethical subject has to be apriori equal to the demand that is placed on it otherwise it would lapse into heteronomy.

In my view, the problem of the fact of reason is the index of a dilemma that determines and arguably divides post-Kantian philosophy. The claim at the basis of the fact of reason is that in order to deal with the problem of motivation, interest or practicability, there has to be a moment of facticity within reason, although this facticity is not the empirical moral feeling of Hutcheson or Hume, but the pure feeling of respect or reverence for the moral law, an apriori feeling. Now, crucially, although reason has to include this moment of facticity within itself in order to explain the problem of motivation, this fact cannot itself be explained. This is the problem that Kant wrestles with in the final, agonised paragraphs of the *Grundlegung*. Philosophically throwing his hands in the air, Kant writes, '*how pure reason can be practical* – all human reason is totally incapable of explaining this, and all the effort and labour to seek such an explanation is in vain'.[21] In other words, we have to accept that the universality of moral law should interest us without being able to explain the cause of that interest. That is to say – and mark the strangeness of this claim – that all we can comprehend of the determination of our will by freedom is its incomprehensibility.

Now, the question is whether this incapacity of explanation is a weakness or a strength. For Fichte, it is a weakness and he attempts to unify theoretical and practical reason through a notion of intellectual intuition. The latter, however, is nothing particularly occult. Rather, Fichte's argument is simply that the moral law becomes internalized in the subject and moral autonomy takes place in and as the self-reflective activity of the subject. He writes, 'Intellectual intuition is the immediate consciousness that I act and of what I do when I act.'[22] For Fichte, intellectual intuition is the self-consciousness of oneself as active; 'Without self-consciousness there is no consciousness whatsoever, but self-consciousness is possible only in the way we have indicated: I am only active.'[23] One might say that Fichte replaces Kant's fact of reason with an act of reason. But rather than seeing this as a critique of Kant, and despite all of Kant's protestations against the possibility of intellectual intuition, Fichte sees the basic principle of his *Wissenschaftslehre* as entirely consistent with the fundamental, animating principle of Kant's system. Fichte asks, 'For Kant would certainly maintain that we are conscious of the categorical imperative, would he not?' And he goes on, 'Our consciousness of the categorical imperative is undoubtedly immediate, but it is not a form of sensory consciousness. In other words, it is precisely what I call "intellectual intuition".'[24] Intellectual intuition is obviously not sensuous intuition. However, nor is it intuition of a metaphysical entity of some kind, like God or the soul. Rather, intellectual intuition is simply the self-intuiting of the subject as active, more specifically as actively determining itself by and through the categorical imperative. Intellectual intuition in Fichte *is* the consciousness of the moral law. The facticity of reason becomes the activity of the subject.

Hegel also rejects the Kantian version of moral insight in the strongest terms as that 'cold duty, the last undigested lump (*Klotz*) in our stomach, a revelation given to reason'.[25] He criticizes Fichte and locates moral autonomy not in the self-awareness of the activity of the subject but in relations of *intersubjectivity* which are constituted by a struggle for recognition.[26] Following Terry Pinkard's reading, we might say that Hegel *socializes* Kantian practical reason.[27] On a Hegelian view, the dilemma at the heart of the Kantian project takes the following form: how can I be subject to a law of which I am the author, given that I can *only* be legitimately subject to such a law because of the governing principle of autonomy. Hegel shows how this Kantian dilemma requires an intersubjective solution, namely that it is necessary to show, firstly, that reason is social, and secondly, that the sociality of reason unfolds historically and cannot be reduced to the formal decision procedure of the Kantian categorical imperative or the solitary activity of the Fichtean ego.

We might also mention Marx in this connection. When Marx writes in the famous eleventh thesis on Feuerbach that 'philosophers have only interpreted the world in different ways, the point however is to change it',[28] what he means is that practical reason must be located in actual praxis, in shared human life. This is what Marx will call, with an implicit nod back to Fichte, 'subjectivity' or 'living activity'. For Marx, the philosophical and political task is the location, description and auto-emancipation of a group who will make philosophy practical and make praxis philosophical. This is the role he assigns to the proletariat who are designated as the universal class and the index of humanity. If Hegel socializes autonomy, then Marx communizes it, where the Kantian kingdom of ends moves from being a postulate of practical reason to an actual realm on earth without kings. Of course, this does not mean that Marx's profession of materialism removes him from the idealist tradition with its focus on the question of autonomy. On the contrary, what we might call Marx's 'materialism of practice' can be seen as the consummation of that tradition that locates autonomy in the life-practice of the proletariat who are what Etienne Balibar calls 'the people of the people' (*le peuple du peuple*), the party of humanity.[29]

Counter-intuitive as it might appear, one can find the inheritance of the Kantian problem of the fact of reason in Heidegger's analysis of the conscience of Dasein or the human being in *Being and Time*. The experience of conscience is that of a call (*Ruf*) or appeal (*Anruf*) which seems to come from outside Dasein, but which is really only Dasein calling to itself. Heidegger writes, '*In conscience Dasein calls itself.*'[30] In this sense, the structure of ethical experience in the early Heidegger, at least in the analysis of authenticity, is an existential deepening of Kantian autonomy. When I pull myself out of the slumber of my inauthentic existence and learn to approve the demand of conscience, which for Heidegger is the demand of my finitude confronted in being-towards-death, then I become authentic, I become who I really am. This is what Heidegger means by 'resoluteness' (*Entschlossenheit*), which is best understood as a form of *autarchy*, self-legislation or self-origination. Heidegger recognizes as a 'positive necessity' the *Faktum* that has to be presupposed in any analysis of Dasein. The Kantian fact of reason becomes, in Heideggerese, the ontic testimony or attestation (*Zeugnis*) of conscience. Crucially, Dasein is not determined by reason, but rather in terms of a pre-rational realm of moods (*Stimmungen*) and a basic mood (*Grundstimmung*) of anxiety, but the autarchic structure of authentic Dasein is an existential echo of the Kantian subject.[31]

Other examples could be given, but the point is that for Fichte, Hegel, Marx and Heidegger and their many heirs in the philosophical tradition, the philosophical goal remains some conception of autonomy, whether the individual ego, individualized Dasein, the intersubjectively constituted realm of Spirit, the collective praxis of the proletariat as the index of humanity, or whatever. Let's say that post-Kantian philosophy, from left to right, from Marx to Heidegger, is dominated by what we might call the autonomy orthodoxy.[32]

Another possible line of inheritance from Kant that I would like to open in the construction of a model of the ethical subject takes precisely the opposite course from the autonomy orthodoxy. This approach would see the moment of ineliminable facticity in Kantian moral reflection as a strength rather than a weakness. On such a view, what Kant implicitly acknowledges in the doctrine of the fact of reason is that the discovery of the philosopher's stone is dependent upon the experience of a demand that halts the philosopher in their tracks and prevents the possession of any miraculous stone. The self confronts a *Faktum* that places an overwhelming demand upon it, and in relation to which it shapes itself as an ethical subject, yet that *Faktum* seems to resist being either explained or understood. As Kant acknowledges in the paradoxical penultimate sentence of the *Grundlegung* alluded to above, 'While we do not comprehend the practical unconditioned necessity of the moral imperative, we do comprehend its *incomprehensibility*.'[33] It is this moment of incomprehensibility in ethics that interests me, where the subject is faced with a demand that does not correspond to its autonomy: in this situation, I am not the equal of the demand that is placed on me. I will now go on to discuss various beneficiaries of this alternative inheritance, whether it is the face of the other person in Levinas, the unfulfillable and one-sided character of the ethical demand in Løgstrup, or the relation to the real in Lacan. For each of them – and us – ethics is obliged to acknowledge a moment of rebellious heteronomy that troubles the sovereignty of autonomy.

2

Dividualism – how to build an ethical subject

We never know self-realization.
We are two abysses – a well staring at the sky.
Fernando Pessoa, *The Book of Disquiet*

Let me review where we have got to in the argument of this book. I began by laying out how I see philosophy beginning in disappointment. That is, philosophy, modern post-Kantian philosophy, begins not in an experience of wonder at what is, but from an experience of failure and lack. One senses that things are not simply wonderful. The two main forms of disappointment analyzed here are religious and political: religious disappointment provokes the question of meaning (what is the meaning of life in the absence of a transcendent deity who would act as a guarantor of meaning?) and opens the problem of nihilism; political disappointment provokes the question of justice (how is justice possible in a violently unjust world?) and provokes the need for an ethics.

In the Introduction, I engaged in a little *Zeitdiagnose* and tried to paint a picture of the present age. I considered a couple of coherent, tempting, but in my view deeply misguided, diagnoses of our times, social pathologies if you prefer. I labelled them 'active nihilism', where I talked about those who seek a violent destruction of the purportedly meaningless world of capitalism and liberal democracy; and 'passive nihilism', where I discussed forms of

'European or American Buddhism', contemplative withdrawal, where one faces the meaningless chaos of the world with eyes wide shut. I rejected both forms of nihilism, but suggested that each of them expresses a deep truth: namely, their identification of a motivational deficit at the heart of liberal democracy, a sort of drift, disbelief and slackening that is both institutional and moral. In the drift of this deficit, we experience the moral claims of our societies as externally compulsory, but not internally compelling. We approach ethical issues in a spirit of Diogenean cynicism rather than free commitment, a spirit in which, as Yeats writes, the best lack all conviction, whilst the worst are full of passionate intensity. The question, then, is how might we fill the best with passionate intensity? I claimed that what was required to deal with this motivational deficit was a motivating, empowering ethics of commitment and political resistance.

What we need to start thinking about in order to begin to make up that deficit is a motivating theory of the ethical subject. On the view argued for in the previous chapter, an ethical subject is the name for the way in which a self binds itself to some conception of the good, whatever that good might be, whether it is Kantian, Sadeian or something in between. At the core of ethical subjectivity is a theory of what I call ethical experience, which is based in two concepts: approval and demand. My basic claim is that ethical experience begins with the approval of a demand, a demand that demands approval. Ethical experience is virtuously circular. The nature of this demand varies in different thinkers: in Plato, it is the demand of the Good beyond Being, for Paul and Augustine it is the demand of the resurrected Christ, for Kant it is the demand of the moral law which is felt as the fact of reason, for Fichte the fact of reason becomes an act of the subject, for Rousseau it is the demand of the suffering human other, for Schopenhauer, it is compassion for all creatures, and so on and so forth. I illustrated the motivational deficit in morality with an extended discussion of the relation of moral justification to motivation in Kant as his work constitutes a *locus classicus* for the problem I am trying to address: namely, how a self binds itself to whatever it determines as its good. Through an analysis of the concept of the fact of reason, I tried to show the fragile necessity at the heart of Kant's claim for the primacy of practical reason and how this claim is taken up by contemporary Kantian philosophers. I concluded with some remarks about what I called the 'autonomy orthodoxy' in post-Kantian philosophy and began to question the sufficiency of autonomy in our ethical thinking.

The task for this chapter is clear: the construction of a model of the ethical subject bearing in mind the stipulations on the notion of 'construction' that I mentioned above. I'm going to take three concepts from three thinkers and then raise a question that I will try and answer in the next chapter on the problem of sublimation. From Alain Badiou, I am going to take the idea of the subject committing itself in fidelity to the universality of a demand that opens in a singular situation but which exceeds that situation. From Knud Ejler Løgstrup, I take the idea of what he calls 'the ethical demand' and his emphasis on the radical, unfulfillable and one-sided character of that demand and the asymmetry of the ethical relation that it establishes. From Emmanuel Levinas, I will try to show how this moment of asymmetry that arises in the experience of the infinite demand of the other's face defines the ethical subject in terms of a split between itself and a exorbitant demand that it can never meet, the demand to be infinitely responsible. So, my normative claim, if you will, is that at the basis of any ethics should be a conception of ethical experience based on the exorbitant demand of infinite responsibility. Not only that, I will also recommend that this exorbitant demand of which I approve is that in relation to which the ethical subject should form itself. The subject shapes itself in relation to a demand that it can never meet, which divides and sunders the subject, the experience of what I will call 'hetero-affectivity', as opposed to the 'auto-affection' of the autonomy orthodoxy.

Before turning to Badiou, my model of ethical experience can be extended to other Francophone thinkers, such as Jean-François Lyotard, where his rather problematic notion of 'the jews' ('*les juifs*'), plays precisely this role of an ethical demand, and where Lyotard also accentuates the moment of heteronomy in Kant through his retrieval of the category of the sublime.[1] It might also be extended to Michel Foucault's late work, specifically Volumes 2 and 3 of *The History of Sexuality*.[2] Although the question that ostensibly guides Foucault's late work is how sexuality was constituted as a moral domain in the classical Greek world and late antiquity, what really interests him is the manner in which one forms oneself as a subject of morality. Ethics is a work of self-formation where the subject, as it were, subjects itself to certain practices which processually aim at a certain *telos*, such as self-mastery, happiness or, for Foucault himself, freedom. Responding to the demand of freedom, Foucault's late thought can be seen as the cultivation of forms of ethical subjectivity capable of resisting the normalizing power of the state and its disciplinary apparatus.[3] Compelling as it is, I do not see Foucault's approach to the ethical subject as decisively breaking with what I called above 'the autonomy orthodoxy'. What marks out his approach is the need for a more embedded, practice-based account of autonomy: care of the self as a practice of freedom. Although it is not my direct concern here, it would also be interesting to extend this theory of ethical experience into contemporary analytic moral theory, whether consequentialism, deontology or virtue ethics. We have looked at a couple of contemporary Kantian moral philosophers, but we might also consider a more Aristotelian approach, such as that given by Sabina Lovibond in her *Ethical Formation*, which draws on McDowell's work on virtue ethics, where she wants to ground moral rationality in the experience of the formation of a self in a process of socialization, what she calls 'authorship'.[4]

Alain Badiou – situated universality

Let me begin with Badiou, whose work has only in recent years begun to attract the attention that it merits in the English-speaking world. His splendid short book, *Ethics – An Essay on the Understanding of Evil*, falls into two parts, one polemical and the other conceptually constructive.[5] In the polemical first part, Badiou takes issue with the so-called 'return to ethics' that has been a feature of French philosophy since the late 1970s as a response to both the foundering of revolutionary Marxism and a pervasive psychoanalytic or structuralist-inspired anti-humanism. In the first chapter of *Ethics*, Badiou criticizes 'les nouveaux philosophes', like André Glucksmann and Bernard Henri-Levy, whose defence of ethics, democracy and human rights is seen as an insipid return to Kantian liberalism. In the second chapter, Badiou attacks Levinas and the extraordinary inflation of ethics based on the category of the Other. For Badiou, Levinasian ethics is simply religion by another name and he sees it – together with the return to Kant – as a symptom of a more general nihilism.

In the constructive second part to the book, Badiou provides a quite other meaning to ethics by relating it not to abstractions, like God, Man or the Other, but to concrete *situations*. In an intriguing echo of Sartre, the category of situation is at the centre of Badiou's ethical theory. If the problem with the ethics of 'Man' or 'the Other' (Kant or Levinas) is the abstract universality of these concepts, then Badiou's remedy is not some concrete relativism, but rather what I would call a *situated universality*. The subject commits itself ethically in terms of a demand that is received from that situation, for example a situation of political injustice: a strike, an act of police brutality, a miscarriage of justice or whatever. But this demand is not reducible to the situation. It is, rather, a situated demand that is addressed, in principle, to everyone and hence universal. To pick an example from the activism of the Parisian political group with which Badiou is affiliated, *L'organisation poli-*

tique, the demand that flows from the situation of the discrimina-
tory treatment of immigrant workers in Paris by the city authorities
is a general claim for equality that exceeds that situation.

However, where one would usually expect to speak about
universality as the means of *justification* for norms of action, what
is most provocative about Badiou's ethics of situations is that he
describes it as an ethics of *truths*. Truths are understood as durable
and non-relativistic maxims for singular and determinate processes, what Badiou calls 'processes of truth'. To return to the
above example, to be committed over a period of time to seeking
equal treatment, rights and benefits for immigrant workers in Paris
is a process of truth. As Raymond Geuss points out in a very helpful
review of Badiou's *Ethics*, 'true' does not mean the property of a
proposition that could be tested or scientifically verified. Rather,

> The basic sense of 'true' is that in which Jesus says of himself that he
> is the truth. To say that Jesus is the truth is to say that his life is the
> true life, i.e. the good life, the exemplary life, the life that is a model
> for humans, the life to which we all should aspire to be faithful.[6]

We will come back to Jesus presently, but note that 'true' is here
being used in a manner close to its root meaning of 'being true to'
or 'troth', namely an act of fidelity that is kept alive in the German
treu, loyal or faithful. For Badiou, truth is 'the real process of fidelity
to an event'.[7] One is true to a demand insofar as one persists in
being faithful to its summons.

Against the 'return to ethics' in French philosophy, Badiou poses
three theses:

1. That ethical subjectivity takes shape through an affirmative
   thinking – in Nietzsche's sense 'active' rather than 'reactive' –
   that consists in the construction of what Badiou calls '*verités
   singulières*', in truths that arise from and apply to singular
   situations.

2. It is from this affirmative character of ethical subjectivity and its ethics of truths that one is able to determine, and determine *positively*, the good. Namely, Badiou adopts the Platonic view that evil is derived from the good by privation, and not *vice versa* – which is a view that he rather mysteriously attributes to Kant. Badiou reads Kantian ethics, with Hegel (although much more simplistically), as a form of ethical stoicism in an evil world devoid of value. The worry is that latter-day Kantianism turns all human beings into rights-claiming *victims* of an evil that is beyond their control. Badiou is very much against what he calls an ethical ideology rooted in the existence of the purportedly 'radical evil' exemplified in the Holocaust.

3. Badiou writes, 'All humanity enroots itself in the identification in thought of singular situations.'[8] That is, there is no ethics in general, there is only an ethics of processes whereby one confronts possible courses of action in a specific situation.

In terms of my theory of ethical experience, Badiou's ethics is an entirely formal theory, a grammar of moral insight, and not a specific determination of the good. However, what is motivating this formalism is a theory of the subject that has strong normative significance – expressed in Badiou's oft-cited words of Beckett, '*il faut continuer*', 'one must go on' – although the specific content given to the good is subject-relative and situation-specific. Ethics cannot be based on any pre-given account of the subject, because the subject is not something that one is, but is rather something that one becomes. One can only speak of the subject in Badiou as a subject-in-becoming insofar as it shapes itself in relation to the demand apprehended in a situation. Also, the subject is not just the individual and Badiou's ethics is not some sort of affirmative solipsism. A subject – say the subject of a political movement or an avant-garde artistic group – can be a collectivity, a group, a plurality of individuals.

For Badiou, we are simply the kinds of animals claimed by circumstances to become a subject. Now, and this is absolutely crucial to understanding Badiou's work, these circumstances cannot be what there is (*ce qu'il y a*). What there is, what Badiou calls 'being' (*être*), is the sheer multiplicity of the world, a plurality of stuff (facts, states of affairs, etc.) that cannot be reduced to any single organizing principle, like Spirit in Hegel, substance in Spinoza or the multitude in Hardt and Negri. As such, the multiplicity of that which is does not place a claim or demand on the subject. A subject, understood as that which becomes, demands something more, it demands that something happens which supplements its place in that which is or 'being'. Badiou calls this supplement an *event*, hence the founding dualism of his work, being and the event (*l'être et l'événement*), the title of his 1988 magnum opus.[9] Thus, an event is that which calls a subject into existence, into the creation of a truth, whereas 'being' or that which is belongs to the order of knowledge. Badiou is a Platonist and believes that being is ultimately to be explained by mathematics. As he states in the initial thesis of L'*être et l'événement*, '*l'ontologie s'accomplisse historiquement comme mathématique*' ('ontology is accomplished historically as mathematics').[10]

The structure of ethical experience in Badiou can be seen in a particularly pure form in his book on Saint Paul from 1997: *Saint Paul. La fondation de l'universalisme*.[11] *Prima facie*, it might well seem odd for a devout atheist like Badiou to concern himself with the founder of the Christian church, but what interests Badiou in Paul is the connection between the subject and the event. More precisely, Badiou's question is: what law can structure a subject in relation to an event, 'of which the only "proof" is rightly that a subject declares it' ('*dont la seule "preuve" est justement qu'un sujet le déclare*'). Of course, for Paul, this event is the resurrection of Christ, something that can only have the status of a fable for an atheist like Badiou. Let me emphasize here, in relation to Badiou's founding dualism of being and the event, that what interests him is the notion of an event which is not empirically demonstrable in the order of being. The event demands an act of faith that Paul rightly compares to folly. That is, the event is, in my terms, a *Faktum* that is analogous but irreducible to an empirical *Tatsache*.

The structure of ethical experience in Badiou's reading of Paul can be formalised into the following four moments: *grace, faith, love* and *hope*.

1. There is the universality of the demand of the good, or what Badiou calls the *adresse*, which is what Paul calls grace, *charis*.
2. The *charisma* or 'gracefulness' of the subject consists in the declaration of this grace in an act of faith, or what Badiou prefers to call *la conviction*, conviction. Thus, faith is the arising or coming forth of the subject (*surgir du sujet*), a subjective certitude that approves of the demand that is placed on it.
3. If faith is *le surgir du sujet*, then love (*agape*) is the practical labour of the subject (*labeur du sujet*) that has bound itself to its good in faith. The practical maxim of love is 'love your neighbour as yourself'. That is, if the human being is justified by faith, then s/he is redeemed by love. Love is what gives consistency to an ethical subject, which allows it to persevere with a process of truth.
4. Love binds itself to justice on the basis of hope. The hope is that justice will be done and the subjective maxim that this requirement of justice produces is, as elsewhere in Badiou, Beckett's 'Continuez!' That is, continue in your conviction and love your neighbour as yourself. That is, we might define hope as *political love*.

It is the first two moments of this structure that are essential in relation to my theory of ethical experience. We begin with the experience of a demand or address, which is the event of grace, and the subject defines itself by approving of this event in a declaration of faith. Thus – and this is essential – *the Christian subject does not pre-*

exist the event that it declares. Subject and event come into being at the same time. The time of Christianity is the present, or rather the eternity of the present, where the subject comes into existence in a relation of identification with the living presence of Christ. Matters are very different in Judaism, where the event – the law, *Torah* – precedes the subject: i.e. I am always already bound by the covenant insofar as I am Jewish. The time of Judaism is the past, what Levinas refers to as the trace of God as a past that has never been present. Yet, this past of the covenant is structurally connected with the future, the future which breaks through the present, the future into which the Messiah might at each moment come.

The subject defines itself by binding itself approvingly, in trothful truth, to the demand that the event makes upon it. For Badiou, but equally for Slavoj Žižek, it is this feature of Pauline Christianity, its universality based on the situated *Faktum* of an event that cannot be reduced to any empirical *Tatsache*, that provides an exemplary figure for contemporary political militantism.[12] It is a question of Paul's activist nomadism against the vast imperial war machine of Rome (and the analogy between the Roman empire and the contemporary American empire, under attack from barbarians, is clear to see). In radical distinction from the politics of government and state administration, politics is here understood as a non-state, non-party based form of activism that begins from the real situations in which people find themselves. Politics is an activity of thought that is directed to an event that takes place in a singular situation.[13] Yet, as I explained above, what is profiled in that event is an ethical universality that exceeds the situation. I will come back to this line of thought when I discuss the passage from ethics to politics in my final chapter.

I have some reservations about Badiou's work. They concern his rather dogmatic attempt to exclude religion as one of the conditions for an event (there are only four conditions for the event: mathematics, politics, art and love), his questionable use of Lacanian psychoanalysis in explaining the relation between subject and event, and a certain *heroism* of the decision that I detect in Badiou, particularly in his political pronouncements.[14] Most significantly, I have reservations about Badiou's talk of truth. The argument here can be broken down into three steps:

1. The logic of the event in Badiou is that an event is that which makes a demand on a subject, *of* which the subject approves and *to* which it decides to bind itself, to be faithful.
2. If step 1 is right, then the logic of the event is circular, not viciously but virtuously; subject and event are equiprimordial concepts with a common and mutually dependent genesis.
3. But if step 2 is right, then why speak of the event as an event of truth? What does truth mean here? Well, according to Badiou and his epigones, truth means that the event is addressed to all, that it has potential universalizability.[15] True equals true for all. But why is this a definition of truth? If truth is here some correspondence between subject and event, then this is obviously mutually entailed by step 2 and is therefore either tautologous or banal or both, i.e. the subject equals the subject of an event and an event equals an event for a subject. But if what is meant by truth is the procedure by which norms are justified, as I think it has to be, then I think it would be better to speak of justification rather than truth, at least in the realm of ethics.

I don't think that truth is a particularly useful or plausible concept in ethics, unless one is some sort of moral realist and Badiou is clearly not playing in that language game. Replacing talk of truth with that of justification, I would say that an event is justified if and only if it is universalizable, that is, if it is in principle addressed to all. An obvious objection that can be made to Badiou is the following: what is the difference between a true and non-true event? Badiou's response is that an event is true if it is addressed to all, which is incidentally why National Socialism cannot have the status of an event because it was not addressed to all, but only to the German *Volk*. True events are those addressed to all, as for example in the claim for equality that is revealed in the unequal treatment received by immigrant workers in France, Britain or the hugely impressive mobilization of immigrant workers across the USA in opposition to repressive proposed legislation in 2006. In my view, however, truth is just what Wittgenstein would call a *way of talking*, and furthermore it is a way of talking about the justification of moral claims. It just sounds more impressive than justification.

Yet, despite these reservations, what grips me in Badiou's work is his account of the relation of subject to event. This permits ethics to be approached as a subjective process or, better perhaps, a process of the formation of ethical subjectivity, where a self *commits* itself with fidelity to a concrete situation, a singular occurrence that places a demand on the self. Yet, this emphasis on the singular and the concrete does not entail relativism, but rather a situated universalism where an event can only be justitifed if it is addressed to all. My commitment to the situation motivates ethical action whose justification exceeds that situation and works to bring about its transformation and amelioration. For me, Badiou's work allows us to breathe life back into the seemingly *caduque* category of *commitment*. In my opinion, Badiou's ethics goes some way to making up on the motivational deficit in morality discussed above.

Knud Ejler Løgstrup – the unfulfillable demand

It is perhaps no accident that Badiou chooses Paul's vision of the resurrected Christ as his paradigm of the event that summons the subject. Christ is the living presence or *parousia* of the divine and one becomes a Christian by an elective participation in this presence, whether through a vision, a revelation, a miracle, the act of eucharist or the simple reading of scripture, if one is Protestant. The time of Christianity is the present and anyone can become Christian by pledging themselves to this event, by committing oneself in faith *now* through a passionate identification with Christ's Passion. For Badiou, the event takes place in the present and the subject pledges itself to that event in the present and enters into a new process of truth. Although it is presumably not meant literally, Badiou even describes the capacity for the true as the 'immortal being' ('*être immortel*') of each subject. For all his avowed atheism, might one not have the suspicion that although Badiou's account of the ethical subject is not substantially Christian in any metaphysical sense, it is still *structurally Christian*?

Yet, if Badiou's work might be structurally Christian, then Levinas's work can aforticia be described as *structurally Judaic*. If Christianity privileges the present where contact with the divine is mediated through the presence of the Son, Jesus Christ, then Judaism privileges the past expressed in the covenant with the Father on Sinai. What does it mean to be Jewish? For Levinas, being Jewish is a *fact* about oneself that cannot be changed. It can either be acknowledged or denied. One can live as a religious or secular Jew, or one can refuse to acknowledge that fact. The point is that neither path changes the fact that one *is* a Jew. One can be a Jew despite oneself. Here one finds an interesting and radical difference from Christianity: anyone can convert themselves to Christianity, or Islam for that matter, by a simple declarative act: 'I am now a Christian', or 'Allahu Akbar'. Matters are not so straighforward with Judaism, which has never been a proselytizing religion and has never sought to convert non-Jews. The event in relation to which the Jewish subject constitutes itself is not the eternal presence of Christ in which one can participate through an act of communion, it is rather the acknowledgement of a fact about the past, of what Levinas sees as the dimension of 'facticity' to which one is bound whether one likes it or not.[16]

However, before turning to Levinas in a little more detail, I would like to examine a rather different interpretation of the ethical demand in Christianity. Løgstrup's relevance for this book can be rather obviously inferred from the title of his important 1956 book, *The Ethical Demand*.[17] Løgstrup and Levinas were almost exact contemporaries, they studied at Strasbourg and Freiburg at the same time and were both exposed to similar philosophical influences such as Bergson, Husserl and Heidegger. In many ways, what makes Løgstrup's work fascinating is the fact that he presents a similar philosophical position to Levinas but from within the Christian tradition. Again, like Levinas, his conception of ethics runs against the current of the major traditions in moral theory, such as Kantianism or any teleological conception of morality, whether utilitarian or Aristotelian. On a Kantian view, I act out of duty for no other reason than duty itself, whereas on a teleological view I act for the sake of the greatest happiness of the greatest number or some conception of *eudaimonia*. For Løgstrup, on the contrary, what the ethical demand requires is that I act for the sake of this living particular human being in front of me: my neighbour, whether stranger or familiar, friend or foe. Løgstrup's understanding of Christianity is that the individual's relation to God is determined *wholly* at the point of his relation to the neighbour. Therefore, one's existence is completely at stake in the relation to the other person and to fail the other is to fail that existence irreparably. However, this emphasis on the lived, existential dimension of ethical experience does not entail that Løgstrup's position is existentialist or Kierkegaardian. Against the existentialist emphasis on radical choice as the basis for one's moral projects, Løgstrup insists that the ethical demand that faces the individual subject in a situation is independent of and prior to subjective choice. In his rather questionable polemic against Kierkegaard, Løgstrup argues that faith is not a subjective matter but is orientated around the 'objectivity' of the demand.

So, what is the ethical demand for Løgstrup? It is Christ's utterly exorbitant demand in the Sermon on the Mount. Although

Løgstrup nowhere cites the scriptural text, I think the following is the passage he has in mind,

> Ye have heard that it hath been said, Thou shalt love thy neighbour, and hate thine enemy.
> But I say unto you, Love your enemies, bless them that curse you, do good to them that hate you, and pray for them which despitefully use you, and persecute you:
> That ye may be the children of your Father which is in heaven: for he maketh his sun to rise upon the evil and on the good, and sendeth rain on the just and on the unjust.
> For if ye love them which love you, what reward have ye? Do not even the publicans the same? And if ye salute your brethren only, what do ye more *than others?* Do not even the publicans so?
> Be ye therefore perfect, even as your Father which is in heaven is perfect. (Matthew 5:43–8, King James translation)

This is a ridiculous demand! Just consider for a moment what Christ is saying to his audience: you might have heard the wisdom of Leviticus that you should love your neighbour as yourself, but that is not enough, you should also love your enemies, you should love those who curse, despise, hate and willfully persecute you. One imagines Carl Schmitt's ears burning. Christ's argument here is that if you love only those who love you in return, then you are not open to the more radical demand of the stranger, the foreigner, the adversary. If you love only your own brethren, the people of your tribe, nation or community, then you are no better than the publicans, the *publicani*, those docile servants of Gentile oppressors who dutifully do whatever the Romans ask of them. What Christ demands of his audience, which is – unless it might be forgotten – a Jewish audience, is that if they wish to be truly the children of their Father, God, then they must subject themselves to this exorbitant demand. That is, Christ is asking his audience to be perfect, god-like, 'even as your Father which is in heaven'.

Of course, such an ethical demand is profoundly paradoxical: can a human being achieve divine perfection? Obviously not. Yet, it is precisely the paradoxical character of the demand that interests Løgstrup for it emphasizes its radicality. One finds a similar logic in Christ's arguments about the nature of forgiveness. When he is asked how many times a person should forgive his or her brother, Christ answers: not seven times, but seventy times seven. This is why Løgstrup describes the demand as not just radical, but as unfulfillable and one-sided. To fulfil the demand would be to become God, which is hardly likely. It is one-sided because it makes an asymmetrical claim – I am not the equal of the demand that is made upon me and the ethical relation is not a relation of equals. As Løgstrup writes in words which could be those of Levinas, 'Responsibility for the other person never consists in our assuming the responsibility which is his or hers'.[18] Responsibility does not here imply reciprocity. On the contrary, the other person always stands higher than oneself. Using a word that recalls our discussion of Kant, Løgstrup continually describes the source of the ethical demand as a *fact*, what we will describe below as *the fact of the other* rather than the fact of reason.[19]

Christ is asking for the impossible, he is articulating a demand that cannot, by definition, be met by fallible, finite human creatures. One might also argue that it is a demand that cannot reasonably be made by one human being to another. This is indeed true: it is utterly unreasonable for one person to demand that another be god-like. Unless, of course, that person is God. To the believer, Christ is not just a human being, but also divine and therefore the living embodiment of the paradox of the finite and the infinite.

Does this mean that Løgstrup's ethics is theological? Does his account of the ethical demand require the acceptance of belief in God, more specifically the divinity of Jesus Christ? These are more delicate questions than might at first appear. Obviously, as I have said, Løgstrup is trying to make sense of the radical ethical demand at the heart of Christ's teaching. Yet, I have also argued that, for Løgstrup, the entire meaning of Christianity is that the individual's relation to God is determined wholly at the point of his relation to the neighbour. Therefore, to be Christian on this view does not mean subscribing to whatever variety of more or less obscure metaphysical beliefs in the incarnation, resurrection or whatever. It means rather that one's entire existence should be organized around the fact of the ethical demand insofar as that demand is enacted in the relation to the other person. Religion is ethics. In this regard, Løgstrup's views on Christ's divinity are extremely interesting. The question of whether it is God himself that we meet in the person of Jesus of Nazareth is something that ultimately, he insists, cannot be decided.[20] What interests Løgstrup is not the nicely intractable theological issue of Christ's divinity, but the fact that Jesus makes an exorbitant demand in an act of preaching, that is, in an address from one individual to another. What we learn from Jesus's words and works is that our existence should be shaped by the approval of the radical, one-sided, unfulfillable ethical demand of the other, and to fail the other is to fail that existence irreparably.

In this connection, Hans Fink and Alasdair MacIntyre write, rightly in my view:

> Løgstrup did indeed take the ethical demand to be that which was commanded by Jesus when he repeated the injunction of *Leviticus* to love our neighbour as ourselves. But for Løgstrup . . . the ethical demand is not laid upon Christians rather than non-Christians. There is not Christian morality *and* secular morality. There is only human morality.[21]

The core of Løgstrup's teaching is that human morality requires responsivity to the ethical demand, an approval of the demand that is experienced in relation to another living person, the neighbour, whether friend or foe. What this entails, interestingly I think, is that the ethical demand is phenomenologically the same for the secularist or the theist. I experience a radical demand and try to shape my subjectivity in relation to it. Whether the demand ultimately emanates from God, the abyssal void at the heart of being, the fairies at the bottom of my garden, or some other occult source is something we cannot know, for good Kantian reasons. The ultimate metaphysical source of ethical obligation, should there be such a thing, is simply not cognizable. In my more extreme view, the question of the metaphysical ground or basis of ethical obligation should simply be disregarded as a philosophical wheel spinning with neither friction nor forward motion. Instead, the focus should be on the radicality of the human demand that faces us, a demand that requires phenomenology and not metaphysics. To put it more paradoxically, knowing that there is no God, we have to subject ourselves to the demand to be God-like, knowing that we are sure to fail because of our finite condition – a godless subjectivation. For Løgstrup, as we have seen, to fail to meet the ethical demand of the neighbour is to fail our existence irreparably. We can now see that such failure is inevitable, for we can never hope to fulfil the radicality of the ethical demand. But far from failure being a reason for dejection or disaffection, I think it should be viewed as the condition for courage in ethical action. The motto for ethical subjectivity is given by Beckett in *Worstward Ho*, 'Try again. Fail again. Fail better.'[22]

What interests me in Badiou is the way in which a subject commits itself in fidelity to the demand that opens in a situation but in a manner which exceeds that situation in the direction of universality. What I take from Løgstrup is his emphasis on the unfulfillable character of the ethical demand and the asymmetry of the ethical relation that it implies. Løgstrup's work can be seen as a questioning of the ethics of autonomy which is obviously dominant in Kant and his epigones and arguably still latent in Badiou's account of the co-originality of subject and event. What is announced in Løgstrup is the possibility of an ethics of heteronomy, or better, a conception of ethical experience which no longer orbits around the auto-affection of the subject, but is articulated through the *hetero-affectivity* of an unfulfillable, one-sided and radical demand. It is this thought that I would like to deepen through a consideration of Levinas's work.

Emmanuel Levinas – the split subject

For Levinas, the core of ethical experience is, indeed, the demand of a *Faktum*, but it is not a Kantian fact of reason so much as what we might call 'a fact of the other'. In *Totality and Infinity*, the name for this fact is the face of the other (*le visage d'autrui*). The ethical relation begins when I experience being placed in question by the face of the other, an experience that happens both when I respond generously to what Levinas, recalling the Hebrew Bible, calls 'the widow, the orphan, the stranger', but also when I pass them by on the street, silently wishing they were somehow invisible and wincing internally at my callousness.

Levinas's difference with Kant is that ethical experience turns around the facticity of a demand that does not correspond to the subject's autonomy, but which rather places that autonomy in question. Ethical experience is heteronomous, my autonomy is called into question by the fact of the other's demand, by the appeal that comes from their face and lays me under an obligation that is not of my choosing. For Levinas, there are two main tendencies in Western philosophy: autonomy and heteronomy. As we saw in the previous chapter, the former has usually been dominant, particularly in the modern period, and Levinas sees his task as the attempt to breathe some life back into the latter. For a philosophy that pursues the project of autonomy, the highest value is that of the subject's freedom, and what must be eliminated, philosophically and socially, is that which stands in the way of freedom. The most extreme expression of this view would be a sort of comic-book version of Hegel which would see history as the progressive realization of freedom. Levinas's claim is that responsibility precedes freedom, that is, prior to the free activity of the subject bringing all of reality within its comprehensive epistemic grasp, there is the experience of a heteronomous demand that calls me into question and calls me to respond. Autonomy comes back into the picture for Levinas at the level of another demand, namely the demand for justice, the just society and everything that he gathers under the heading of 'the third party'. What must be acknowledged is the heteronomous constitution of autonomy, that the ethical demand is refractory to our cognitive powers and the other person can always resist whatever concept under which we may try to subsume them.

In my view, the basic operation of Levinas's entire work is the experience of an exorbitant demand which heteronomously determines the ethical subject. This demand is the imperative *'tu ne tueras point'*, 'you shall not kill', which is expressed in the resistance of the other's face. The demand provokes an act of approval on the part of the subject, the words *'me voici'*, 'here I am', the Hebrew *'hinneni'* of Abraham's response to the demand of God in Genesis 22. Levinas insists that the subject discovers itself as an object, in the accusative case as he puts it, as interlocuted by the demand of the other. But the Levinasian subject is constituted through an act of approval to a demand to which it is fundamentally *inadequate*. I am not the equal of the demand that is made upon me. It is this fundamental inadequacy of approval to demand that explains why, for Levinas, the relation to the other is assymetrical. That is, the subject relates itself to something that exceeds its relational capacity. This is what Levinas paradoxically calls *'le rapport sans rapport'*, the relation without relation, which is arguably the central concept of Levinas's *Totality and Infinity*. Yet, how can there be a relation between beings that remain absolute within that relation? Logically speaking, this is a contradiction in terms, yet it is precisely such a relation that Levinas wants to describe as ethical.

This difficulty can be illuminated by considering the function of the concept of infinity in Levinas's work. From the late 1950s onwards, he describes the ethical relation to the other in terms of infinity. What does this mean? Levinas's claim is very simple, but even quite sophisticated readers still get it muddled. The idea is that the ethical relation to the other has a *formal* resemblance to the relation, in Descartes's Third Meditation, between the *res cogitans* and the infinity of God. What interests Levinas in this moment of Descartes's argument is that the human subject has an idea of infinity, and that this idea, by definition, is a thought that contains more than can be thought. As Levinas puts it, in what is almost a mantra in his published work, 'In thinking infinity the I from the first *thinks more than it thinks*.'[23]

It is this formal structure of a thought that thinks more than it can think, that has a surplus within itself, that intrigues Levinas because it sketches the contours of a relation to something that is always in excess of whatever idea I may have of it, that always escapes me. The Cartesian picture of the relation of the *res cogitans* to God through the idea of the infinite provides Levinas with a picture or formal model of a relation between two terms that is based on height, inequality, non-reciprocity and asymmetry. As he writes, in a characteristic series of antitheses,

> The idea of the infinite consists precisely and paradoxically in thinking more than what is thought while nevertheless conserving it in its excessive relation to thought. The idea of the infinite consists in grasping the ungraspable while nevertheless guaranteeing its status as ungraspable.[24]

However, Levinas is making no substantive claim at this point, he is not saying that I actually *do* possess the idea of the infinite in the way Descartes describes, nor is he claiming that the other is God, as some readers mistakenly continue to believe. As Hilary Putnam rightly points out, 'It isn't that Levinas *accepts* Descartes' argument, so interpreted. The significance is rather that Levinas *transforms* the argument by substituting the Other for God.[25]

As Levinas is a phenomenologist, it becomes a question for him of trying to locate some concrete content for this formal structure. Levinas's major substantive claim, that resounds in different ways throughout his mature work, is that the ethical relation of the self to the other corresponds to this picture, concretely fulfilling this model. One might say that the ethical relation to the face of the other person is the *social* expression of this formal structure. Levinas writes, 'the idea of infinity is the social relationship', and again, 'The way in which the other presents himself, exceeding *the idea of the other in me*, we here name face.'[26] Thus, the ethical relation to the other produces what Levinas calls in a favorite formulation – rightly emphasized by Maurice Blanchot in his writings on Levinas – 'a curvature of intersubjective space'.[27] When I am actually within the ethical relation, I experience the other as the high point of this curvature. As such, the relation can only be totalized by imagining myself occupying some God-like, third-person perspective outside of the relation. From a Levinasian point of view, this is the common shortcoming of various theories of intersubjectivity. For example, Hegel's thesis is that subjectivity is constituted through an intersubjective dialectic, namely the life and death struggle of master and slave. For Husserl, my full constitution as an ego is dependent on a relation to the alter-ego, whereas for Heidegger *Dasein* is *Mitsein*; what it means to be a person is indistinguishable from my being with others. For each of '*les trois H*', as they were called in France, the relation between self and other is a relation of equality, symmetry and reciprocity. Levinas's polemical point is that the relation between myself and the other only appears as a relation of equality, symmetry and reciprocity from a neutral, third-person perspective that stands outside that relation. When I am within the relation, then the other is not my equal and my responsibility towards them is infinite. It is such a non-dialectical model of intersubjectivity that Levinas has in mind, I think, with the notion of the 'relation without relation'.

The picture of ethical experience that I am trying to elicit can be explored by picking out one item in the philosophical vocabulary of Levinas's later work: trauma. What is trauma? Trauma has both a physiological and a psychological meaning, denoting a violence effected by an external agency, which can be a blow to the head as much as the shock of emotional bereavement. As such, a trauma is something that comes from outside the self, the irruption of a heteronomous fact that can strike without warning, like a terrorist explosion. Whence arises the riddle of traumatic neurosis. Traumatic neurosis is the disorder that arises after the experience of a trauma, where its effect lives on at the heart of the subject. Like other neuroses, it is compulsive and repetitive: the original scene of the trauma is obsessively and unconsciously repeated, perhaps in nightmares or insomnia. It is the phenomenon of traumatic neurosis, in the form of shellshock or war-neurosis, that causes Freud such theoretical difficulties in *Beyond the Pleasure Principle*. This is for the simple reason that if there is a compulsion to repeat at work in traumatic neurosis that repeats the origin of trauma, then how can this be consistent with the thesis of Freud's early work that dreams and other psychic phenomena are wish-fulfillments governed by the pleasure principle? It cannot, and it is on the basis of the clinical evidence of traumatic neurosis that Freud is led to introduce the repetition compulsion and to engage in the speculation that he calls 'the death drive'.

What does that have to do with Levinas? In his later work, Levinas constructs what he calls an 'ethical language', composed of several strange, wonderful and hyperbolical terms: persecution, obsession, substitution, hostage and trauma. Levinas makes the extreme claim that my relation to the other is not some benign benevolence, compassionate care or respect for the other's autonomy, but is the obsessive experience of a responsibility that persecutes me with its sheer weight. I am the other's hostage, taken by them and prepared to substitute myself for any suffering and humiliation that they may undergo. I am responsible for the persecution I undergo and even for my persecutor; a claim that, given the experience of Levinas's family and people during the Second World War, is nothing less than extraordinary. Trauma was not a theoretical issue for Levinas, but a way of dealing with the memory of horror. In a number of texts from the late 1960s and 1970s, Levinas describes the relation of infinite responsibility to the other as a trauma. In 'God and Philosophy', he writes,

> This trauma, which cannot be assumed, inflicted by the Infinite on presence, or this affecting of presence by the Infinite – this affectivity – takes shape as a subjection to the neighbour. It is thought thinking more than it thinks, desire, the reference to the neighbour, the responsibility for another.[28]

In short, the Levinasian ethical subject is a traumatic neurotic. I want to focus on the notion of trauma in order to bring out the links between Levinas and the psychoanalytic dimensions of ethical experience that I will come back to below. Although Levinas was extremely hostile towards psychoanalysis and largely ignorant of it, I would like to redescribe Levinas in psycho-analytic terms for reasons that will become clearer when we turn to Lacan. The point here is that, for Levinas, the ethical demand is a traumatic demand, it is something that comes from outside the subject, from a heteronomous source, but which leaves its imprint within the subject. At its heart, the ethical subject is marked by an experience of hetero-affectivity. In other words, the inside of my inside is somehow outside, the core of my sub-jectivity is exposed to otherness.

Ethical experience in Levinas is rooted in the claim that responsibility begins with a subject approving of a demand that it can never meet, a one-sided, radical and unfulfillable demand in Løgstrup's sense. Levinas writes, 'To be I signifies not being able to escape responsibility'; or again, 'to be a "self" is to be responsible before having done anything'.[29] I, as it were, decide to be a subject that I know I cannot be. I give myself up to a demand that makes an imprint upon *me* without my ever being able to understand *it*. 'I' am an existential exaggeration. In language closer to Levinas, this is another way of thinking about what he means by the claim that ethics is not ontology. Arguably, the main thesis of Levinas's work is that the ethical relation to the other is not one of comprehension and cannot therefore be subsumed within Heideggerian *Seinsverständnis*, understanding of being. We can now see how this thesis looks from the perspective of ethical subjectivity: the relation to the other lives on as an imprint in the subject to which it responds but which it cannot comprehend. That is, there is something at the heart of me, that arguably makes me the 'me' that I am, but which is quite opaque to me. This is what I called above, in relation to Kant, the moment of irreducible *facticity* at the heart of the subject.

In my view, and this is a somewhat heterodox claim, the key concept in Levinas's work is ethical subjectivity. The precondition for the ethical relation to the other is found in Levinas's picture of the ethical subject. It is because of a disposition towards alterity at the heart of the subject that relatedness to the other is possible. This is why I tend to privilege Levinas's later work, *Otherwise than Being*, over his earlier work, *Totality and Infinity*, for it is here that ethics is worked out as a theory of the subject, what he calls 'the other within the same'. In terms of the overall argument of this book, commitment or fidelity (Badiou) to the unfulfillable, one-sided and radical demand that pledges me to the other (Løgstrup) can now be seen to be the structure of ethical subjectivity itself (Levinas). The ethical subject is defined by the approval of a traumatic heteronomous demand at its heart. But, importantly, the subject is also *divided* by this demand, it is constitutively *split* between itself and a demand that it cannot meet, but which is that by virtue of which it becomes a subject. The ethical subject is a split subject.

Jacques Lacan – the Thingly secrecy of the neighbour

Levinas and Lacan might seem to be rather odd bedfellows.[30] Yet I want to claim that they identify a common formal structure to ethical experience despite the enormous, doubtless insurmountable, differences between them at the level of content, not the least of which are their starkly antithetical evaluations of the importance of Freud. Putting aside all the jargonistic mouthwash of Lacanianism, let's ask: what is the core claim of Lacan's extraordinarily rich Seminar VII, *The Ethics of Psychoanalysis*?[31] Figure 4 tries to schematize the structure of ethical experience in Lacan. Lacan's thesis is that ethics is articulated in relation to the order of the real:

> My thesis is that the moral law, the moral command, the presence of the moral agency in our activity, insofar as it is structured by the symbolic, is that through which the real is actualized – the real as such, the weight of the real.[32]

The real is variously and obscurely glossed by Lacan as 'that which resists, the impossible, that which always comes back to the same place, the limit of all symbolization'. The basic thought here is that the real is that which exceeds and resists the subject's powers of conceptualization or the reach of its criteria.

This thesis is then finessed in the following crucial way: ethics is articulated in relation to the order of the real insofar as the real is the guarantor of what Lacan calls *das Ding, la Chose*, the Thing. Ethics is a relation to the real and what stands in the place of the real is the Thing. With characteristic self-conscious aplomb, Lacan says:

THE STRUCTURE OF ETHICAL EXPERIENCE IN LACAN

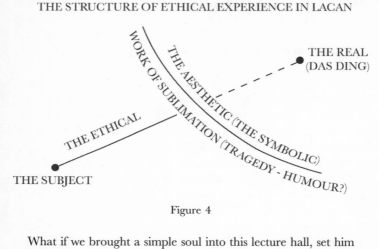

Figure 4

What if we brought a simple soul into this lecture hall, set him down in the front row, and asked him what Lacan means. The simple soul will get up, go to the board, and will give the following explanation: "since the beginning of the academic year Lacan has been talking to us about *das Ding* in the following terms. He situates it at the heart of a subjective world which is the one whose economy he has been describing to us from a Freudian perspective for years".[33]

But what exactly is the Thing? Although Lacan makes allusions to Kant's notion of the thing-in-itself *(Ding-an-sich)* and Heidegger's essay on Kant, *What is a Thing?*, the main example of the Thing in the ethics seminar is Freud's figure of the *Nebenmensch*, the fellow human being or neighbour.[34] But what does it mean to say the fellow human being is the Thing? Lacan's reading of Freud on this point is interestingly idiosyncratic, and everything turns on the interpretation of a single passage from Freud's early 1895 *Project for a Scientific Psychology* that was only published in 1950, but which predicts many of his subsequent metapsychological insights. Lacan focuses on what he says 'remains open or gaping' in Freud's text.[35]

Let me paraphrase the key passage: Freud talks about 'the complex of the fellow human being' or even 'the neighbour complex'. This complex breaks down into two components, Freud says. On the one hand, if I look at another human being, say someone I know well, then there are things about him or her that I understand and that I can describe, such as facial features, mannerisms, tone of voice, etc. However, Freud goes on to claim that there is something about the neighbour that escapes my comprehension and which stands apart from me, *als Ding*, as a Thing. Therefore, as well as I might know someone, even someone I share my life with, there is a dimension of *Thingly secrecy* about them that I cannot know. In his commentary on this passage from Freud, Lacan writes, 'The *Ding* is the element that is initially isolated by the subject in his experience of the *Nebenmensch* as being by its very nature alien, *Fremde*.' And again, 'The world of our experience, the Freudian world, assumes that it is this object, *das Ding*, as the absolute Other of the subject, that one is supposed to find again. It is to be found at the most as something to be missed.'[36] What interests Lacan is the idea of the Thingliness of the other person as something alien to me but which is located at the core of my subjectivity. The Thing is, we might say, the excluded interior, where I discover that what is most interior to my interiority is exterior to me, it is 'something strange to me, although it is at the heart of me'.[37]

The thought here might be expressed more prosaically with reference to the old epistemological chestnut of the problem of other minds. How can I know that another person is truly in pain? In Stanley Cavell's surrealistic restatement of the problem, let's imagine that I am a dentist drilling a patient's tooth and the patient suddenly screams out as a response to what seems like the pain caused by my clumsy drilling. And yet, in response to my embarrassed show of remorse, the patient says, 'It wasn't hurting, I was just calling my hamsters.'[38] Now, how can I know that the other person is being sincere, short of his hamsters scuttling obediently into my dental surgery? The point is that ultimately *I cannot*. I can never *know* whether another person is in pain or simply calling his hamsters. That is to say, there is something about the other person, a dimension of separateness, Thingly secrecy or what Levinas calls 'alterity' that escapes my comprehension. That which exceeds the bounds of my knowledge demands *acknowledgement*.

Leaving hamsters to one side, in my view there is a *Nebenmensch* complex at work in both Levinas and Lacan. For both of them, ethical experience begins with a heteronomous demand, the infinite demand of the other's face in Levinas, the demand of the fellow human being who stands in the place of the real in Lacan. Furthermore, the demand of this Thing lodges itself at the heart of the subject, as something strange to me though it is at the heart of me, as the excluded interior. We might think of the Thing as a traumatic imprint within the subject, the opaque underside of facticity that is at the heart of the subject yet foreign to it.

More generally, it is interesting to note how well the ethics of psychoanalysis fits into the structure of ethical experience and ethical subjectivity that I have tried to describe in this book. One might say that psychoanalytic experience begins with the recognition of the *demand* of the unconscious, the impingement of the *Faktum* of unconscious desire in the form of the symptom. In the analytic situation, that is, if the analysand has *agreed* to the interpretation of the symptom, the *Faktum* of this desire provokes an act of *approval* of the part of the subject. That is, the subject decides henceforth to relate itself approvingly to the demand of its unconscious desire. This demand produces what I see as the categorical imperative of Lacanian ethics and which is the motto of *The Ethics of Psychoanalysis*, 'do not give way on its desire' ('*ne pas céder sur son désir*'). That is, do not cease to approve of the demand of unconscious desire in the activity of its interpretation. For Lacan, it is this act of approval that founds the subject, where he claims that '*tout le cheminement du sujet*', the entire itinerary of the subject, articulates itself around the Thing that casts its shadow across it.[39] Thus, psychoanalysis has the *moral* goal of putting the subject in relation to its desire. This is why Lacan can rightly claim that Freudian psychoanalysis, as much as Kant's critical philosophy, subscribes to the primacy of practical reason. The difference between Lacan and Kant, like that between Levinas and Kant, lies in the gap between the heteronomous and autonomous determinations of the ethical subject. The unconscious is not a law that I willfully give myself, it is a law to which I am involuntarily given. The ethical question is ultimately how I transmute the passion of the unconscious.

However, I am not in the business of trying to foist some sort of arranged marriage upon Levinas and Lacan. My use of psycho-analysis is intended to be critical of Levinas in two important regards:

(i) It is hoped that using Freudian categories to offer a recon-struction of Levinas's work as a theory of the subject minimizes some of the metaphysical residua and religious pietism present in Levinas's texts, but even more present in certain interpretations of those texts. In my view, psycho-analysis provides a non-theological account of the nature of what we called above 'exciting reasons', a vocabulary of desire, affection and the passions.

(ii) Returning to Lacan, it is important to recall that there are two main topics in *The Ethics of Psychoanalysis*: ethics and *sublimation*. Might one not wonder whether Levinas's ethics condemn us to a lifetime of trauma and lacerating guilt that cannot – and, moreover, should not – be worked through? Doesn't Levinas leave us in a situation of sheer ethical overload where I must be responsible even for my perse-cutor, and where the more that I am just the more I am guilty. If so, then such a position risks amounting to nothing less than a rather long philosophical suicide note or at the very least an invitation to some fairly brutal moral masochism.[40] In my view, thinking of the work of Melanie Klein, the trauma of separation requires *reparation*, the ethical *tear* requires *repair* in a work of sublimation that would be a work of love.[41] In other words, Levinas risks producing an ethics without sublimation, which risks being disastrously self-destructive to the subject. This brings us to the topic of the next chapter.

3

The problem of sublimation

The major claim in the last chapter was that there should be a conception of ethical experience at the heart of morality based on the exorbitant demand of infinite responsibility. Not only that, I also claimed that this unfulfillable demand of which I approve is that in relation to which the ethical subject should form itself. Ethics should be infinitely demanding. There is a curvature of intersubjective space that makes my relation to the other asymmetrical. Furthermore, this curvature shapes the inner space of subjectivity itself, where the subject is defined in terms of a division between itself and an exorbitant demand that it can never meet, the demand to be infinitely responsible. The ethical subject shapes itself in relation to a demand that splits it open.

The question that this raises brings to mind Nietzsche's account of the origin of bad conscience in *On the Genealogy of Morals*: namely, doesn't the conception of the ethical subject proposed in this book end up in what Nietzsche would call 'conscience vivisection' and 'self-torture', what Gabriela Basterra has called 'tragic guilt'?[1] How can the extremity of the ethical picture I have described be borne without crushing the ethical subject? How can I respond in infinite responsibility to the other without extinguishing myself as a subject? Doesn't traumatic ethical separation require aesthetic reparation? This, of course, is the topic of *sublimation* and to discuss this we will have to turn again to psychoanalysis, more particularly Lacan, and more particularly still Seminar VII, *The Ethics of*

Psychoanalysis. This will take us firstly into tragedy and then into humour.

Happiness?

What is demanded in psychoanalysis? Lacan's response is unambiguous: *happiness*. However, in the time that separates us from Aristotle, the question of happiness is not amenable to an Aristotelian solution. The ethical life cannot, for we moderns, be said to culminate in the goal of *eudaimonia*, better translated as 'well-goddedness' than as happiness in the modern sense. Although it is not made explicit, there is an implied genealogy of morals in Lacan's work, what he refers to in *The Ethics of Psychoanalysis* as 'the crisis of ethics', a crisis that comes oddly close to Alasdair Mac-Intyre's critical diagnosis of modernity.[2] For Lacan, we can no longer pursue what he calls an aristocratic ethics of the sovereign good. We live in symbolically impoverished societies which have been subject to the disappearance of forms of community where ethics is rooted in *ethos*, in custom, habit and tradition, what Hegel calls *Sittlichkeit*, ethical life. We live, to coin a phrase, after virtue. The idea that one finds in Aristotle or, for that matter Aquinas, that happiness or beatitude is identical with respect for the principles of natural law and therefore ultimately with the will of God, has evaporated. For Lacan, the question of happiness has become what he calls a political matter, a matter for everyone, 'there is no satisfaction apart from the satisfaction of all'. That is, happiness is no longer referable to the position of the master or to be subsumed under the ideal of contemplation, Aristotle's *bios theoretikos*. Rather, happiness is referred to an abstract quantitative generality. It becomes the happiness of the greatest number. Of course, what Lacan is describing here is the Benthamite world of utilitarianism, where happiness becomes the object of a moral calculus. Happiness is simply the maximal satisfaction of our inclinations. This is why Kant, rightly, wants to separate morality from happiness or what he calls 'eudaimonism'.

In such an ethically impoverished world, what possible happiness does psychoanalysis offer? Lacan's response is, once again, quite clear: *sublimation*. Although Freud calls upon the concept of sublimation throughout his work, he offers no overall theoretical account of it. In a short text on Marguerite Duras, Lacan wittily remarks that sublimation is '. . . something that still confounds psychoanalysts because, in handing down the term to them, Freud's mouth remained sewn shut'.[3] Laplanche and Pontalis in *Vocabulaire de la psychanalyse* consider the lack of a coherent theory of sublimation as one of the major lacunae in psychoanalytic thought and I see no reason to disagree.[4] That said, one must acknowledge the important work of Hans Loewald, in particular his *Sublimation*.[5] Loewald beautifully defines sublimation as 'passion transformed', and at the centre of his concerns is the question of the relation of sublimation to guilt, which leads him to a quite fascinating reformulation of the super-ego in its relation to time, which I will come back to below.

In his important paper on narcissism, Freud formulaically defines sublimation as satisfaction without repression. That is, sublimation is the satisfaction of a drive insofar as that drive is deflected from its aim or goal in finding a new object. For example, the sexual drive can be deflected from its aim through religious sublimation, as in the ecstasies of mystics and poets.[6] Following the pathbreaking work of Melanie Klein, whom he doesn't always acknowledge as much as he should, sublimation has, for Lacan, a wider purview than an internal transformation of the sexual drive. It is sublimation in the form of art that interests Lacan, specifically tragedy. Psychoanalysis is tragic knowledge and in the absence of the possibility of happiness, a tragedy confronted on the couch in the form of symptoms, only sublimation can save us, more particularly a thinking of the tragic might save us.

What is the moral goal of psychoanalysis? We have already seen that it cannot consist in putting the subject back into a relation to the sovereign good where virtue would be identical with happiness. But Lacan also dismisses the contemporary *idée fixe* that psychoanalysis might be able to restore some kind of psychological normality, that the subject might be able to readjust to reality by achieving a new harmonization of drive and object. Lacan says that such an idea of the ethics of psychoanalysis is nothing less than 'a kind of fraud', which reduces analysis to what he calls 'the service of goods'. Rather, the moral goal of psychoanalysis consists in putting the subject in relation to its unconscious desire. This is why sublimation is so important, for it is the realization of such desire.

The problematic of desire is pursued in relation to death. Following the later Freud, Lacan sees the death drive as the fundamental aim or tendency of human life. The question of sublimation becomes: how can the human being have access to the death drive? That is, how can one grasp the meaning of human finitude or what Lacan calls, with surprising forthrightness, 'the reality of the human condition'?[7] Lacan's answer is simple: through *beauty*. Sublimation is creative artistic activity that produces beauty and the function of the beautiful is to realize the human being's relation to death. Yet, 'realize' is too strong a verb here, for it is not that the beautiful artwork places the subject in a relation of adequation with the truth of finitude. Desire cannot be realized because that towards which desire tends is death. The realization of desire would require the extinction of the subject. Access to what we might call the real of death is only represented in a work of sublimation that traces an excess within representation. If the relation to the real is the realm of the ethical, and the work of sublimation is the realm of the aesthetic, then we might say that *the aesthetic intimates the excess of the ethical over the aesthetic*.

Hence, the importance of the figure of Antigone and the experience of the tragic in *The Ethics of Psychoanalysis*. Antigone, as Lacan's figure for the beautiful, embodies this excess of the ethical over the aesthetic. The effect of her beauty, what Lacan refers to as her 'splendour', is to trace the sublime movement of the ethical within the aesthetic. The key term in Lacan's extraordinary reading of the *Antigone* is *atè*, which he renders as 'transgression'. Thus, the function of art is transgression, the transgression *of* the aesthetic *through* the aesthetic. Namely, that Antigone transgresses the laws of utilitarian Creon, refuses to feel any guilt for her transgression and does not give way on her desire. As such, she obeys the categorical imperative of Lacanian psychoanalysis: *ne pas céder sur son désir*.

The law of desire is death and Antigone goes all the way unto death because she will not give way on her desire. The beautiful work of sublimation, and Antigone is this work – she *is* the beautiful – takes the human being to the limit of a desire which cannot be fully represented. The work of sublimation traces the outline of something sublime, the aesthetic object describes the contour of the Thing, *la Chose*, *das Ding*, at the heart of ethical experience. In Seminar VII, this is why Lacan writes, 'Thus, the most general formula that I can give you of sublimation is the following: it raises the object to the dignity of the Thing.'[8] In sublimation, we are momentarily lifted from the utilitarian world of calculations, the world of our familiar concerns, and allowed a relation to the Thing that does not crush or destroy us. The beautiful artwork *sublimes* the object, endowing it with Thingly dignity. Or again, beauty sublimes an object into the Thing. In relation to this sublimed object, we experience catharsis, what Lacan thinks of as a kind of purification of desire.

The tragic-heroic paradigm

With these thoughts in mind, take another look at Figure 4. What I want to emphasize is the way in which sublimation produces a kind of aesthetic screen which allows the profile of the Thing to be projected whilst not being adequate to its representation. The aesthetic cuts across the trajectory of the ethical in a way that both places the subject in relation to the source of the ethical demand, but which protects the subject from the direct glare of the Thing. Returning to the distinction I introduced above, on this model we can achieve aesthetic reparation for ethical separation without either losing the radicality of ethical demand or transforming that demand into a form of oppression. Through the experience of sublimation, we can come into contact with the hyperbolic dimension of the ethical demand without that demand crushing the subject.

Let me translate this into Nietzschean categories: we need art lest we might perish from the truth. That is to say, art gives us a glimpse of the truth of finitude, what the early Nietzsche rather rhapsodically expressed as the 'Dionysian womb of being'. This is the wisdom of Silenus, 'What is best of all is utterly beyond your reach: not to be born, not to be, to be nothing. But the second best for you is – to die soon.'[9] But art also saves us from that truth by the beautiful *Schein* or shining semblance of the artwork. For Nietzsche, the distinction of Attic tragedy is that it sets forth this conflict between the Apollinian and the Dionysian, it both reveals the truth of human finitude and it redeems us from that truth. Nietzsche's question, which becomes increasingly questionable to him as his work develops, is whether and in what form the spirit of Attic tragedy can be reborn.

These correspondences between Lacan's and Nietzsche's early views on tragedy should, I think, in no way surprise us. They are both heirs to what Peter Szondi has rightly called 'the philosophy of the tragic' which has an almost uncanny persistence in the German philosophical tradition and which exerts a strong influence in French intellectual life from the 1930s onwards.[10] I won't tell the full story here, which begins with the early Schelling's response to Kant in the *Letters on Dogmatism and Criticism* from 1796. What interests Schelling is the Kantian category of the aesthetic, which is, 'the keystone in the entire arch' of the critical philosophy.

Not only that, tragedy is chosen as the aesthetic genre that can reconcile the freedom of the subject with the causal necessity of the natural world. That is, the category of the aesthetic analysed in Kant's Third Critique is the bridge between the epistemology of the First Critique and the ethics of the Second Critique. Schelling writes,

> The essence of *tragedy* is thus an actual and objective conflict between freedom in the subject on the one hand, and necessity on the other, a conflict that does not end such that one or the other succumbs, but rather such that both are manifested in perfect indifference as simultaneously victorious and vanquished.[11]

Schelling is thinking of Sophocles' *Oedipus Rex* rather than the *Antigone,* and the claim here is that at the end of the tragedy Oedipus succeeds in attaining a free recognition of his determination by necessity or fate. At the start of the drama, Oedipus falsely believed himself to be free. Unbeknownst to himself, however, he is determined by necessity: married to his mother, his father's murderer and the source of the evil pollution that threatens the life of the *polis.* By the end of the tragedy, however, Oedipus is truly free because he knows the truth about who he is and also knows what is to be done, that he must leave the *polis.* Having struck out his eyes, he can finally see and is led calmly from the stage by the hand of his daughter, Antigone. The tragic hero, then, is defined by the free acceptance of their determination by fate. They heroically bear the truth of their finitude in an act of affirmation which allows them to achieve authenticity.[12]

There is a massive and complex privileging of the tragic in post-Kantian Germanophone philosophy, which extends to Hölderlin's translations of Sophocles and his repeated attempts to write his own tragedy, *The Death of Empedocles*; to Hegel's interpretation of the *Antigone* in *Phenomenology of Spirit*, of the *Oresteia* in his early essay

on natural law and his rich understanding of dramatic art in his
Aesthetics; to Nietzsche's early account of the birth and possible
rebirth of tragedy and constant fascination with the idea of tragic
affirmation; through to Freud's development of the Oedipus
complex and thinkers as diverse as Georg Simmel and Max
Scheler. Indeed, one might even claim that post-Kantian philosophy right up to the present suffers from an Antigone complex
with recurrent outbreaks of Hellenomania.[13] For a rather different
angle on Antigone, one might look at Judith Butler's *Antigone's
Claim*.[14] For Butler, far from representing some pure idea of 'the
feminine' or the laws of kinship, as she does for both Hegel and
Lacan in different yet related ways, Antigone represents the
instability, porosity and fragility of gender identity and the utterly
contingent character of social relations and kinship structures. Far
from being one pole in an essentialized concept of sexual difference, Antigone is a kind of anti-generation figure for the emergence of new forms of gender identification and family structure.

What specifically interests me, and what I would like to question,
is the thought that in tragic action the subject can achieve
authenticity in its confrontation with finitude. For Heidegger, this
is the lesson of Sophocles' *Antigone*, and his peculiarly Promethean
interpretation of the drama seems to have exerted no little
influence on Lacan. For Heidegger, the second stasimon of the
Antigone, the famous 'hymn to man', provides not only the 'authentic Greek definition of the human being', but also the basic trait of
what it means to be human, namely to be 'the uncanniest one' (*das
Unheimlichste*), to be a stranger and exile upon the earth.[15] For
Heidegger, like Lacan, the tragic hero is possessed by *atè*, the free
and violent drive for truth that leads them to 'ruin and disaster'.
But the free transgression of the tragic hero is also a necessity
insofar as it is only by opposing the inauthentic life of Creon's
utilitarian *polis* that one can become authentically oneself in facing
up to one's fate in being-towards-death (*Sein-zum-Tode*). For Lacan
too, the relation between action and desire in the space of tragedy

is concerned with what he calls 'a triumph of being-towards-death', which is simply Lacan's rendering of Heidegger's *Sein-zum-Tode*.[16] Lacan's thesis would seem to be that tragedy provides an exemplary model of ethical action in conformity with one's desire insofar as desire is bound up in a relation to death. To my mind, Lacan makes Antigone into the heroine of psychoanalysis: she who does not give way on her desire and follows that categorical imperative all the way to her death. Lacan's reading of the *Antigone* is the psychoanalytic extension of the German philosophy of the tragic.

What is at work in Lacan, at least in *The Ethics of Psychoanalysis*, is a tragic paradigm whose ancestry can be traced at the very least to Heidegger and Schelling. Slavoj Žižek seems to accept my criticism of Lacan's interpretation of the figure of Antigone, arguing that she engages in what he calls, 'the heroic suicidal transgressive gesture which excludes the subject from the symbolic community'.[17] However, he goes on to argue that Lacan's views change significantly in his later work and he replaces the lofty heroic pathos of the relation of the subject to *das Ding* with a more pragmatic pluralism of smaller desires. The best example of the *objet petit a* that causes desire in the subject in late Lacan is, Žižek quips, the difference between \$2.99 and \$3.00. Be that as it may, my claims about Lacan are diagnostic rather than philological and restricted to *The Ethics of Psychoanalysis*.

Humour

What's wrong with the tragic paradigm? In my view, the tragic paradigm distorts the picture of human finitude by making the subject too *heroic*. What do I mean by heroism? That the tragic hero achieves *authenticity* in the relation between action and desire in the experience of being-towards-death. In becoming the uncanniest one, in refusing to give way on their desire and letting their action be prescribed by that desire, the hero rises up into an authentic understanding of their finitude. The tragic hero becomes who they truly are, in Nietzsche's words cited by Heidegger in *Being and Time*. I discuss elsewhere the truly unwholesome political consequences of the tragic-heroic paradigm and its jargon of authenticity, which are all too evident in Heidegger's reading of Sophocles.[18] Basically, the problem with the tragic paradigm is that it implies a heroic model of authenticity. For me, authenticity is not something to be salvaged from the wreckage of Heidegger's existential analytic, in the manner of someone like Charles Taylor or Charles Guignon.[19] On the contrary, I want to argue for a notion of *originary inauthenticity* at the core of subjective experience which opens in relation to the facticity of an ethical demand that I cannot fully comprehend and to which I am not adequate. Let me try to approach this issue by returning to the topic of sublimation which is still needed despite my scepticism about the tragic-heroic paradigm.

My question to the tragic-heroic paradigm is very simple: might there not be other ways of sublimating ethical experience than tragedy? More specifically, might there be forms of sublimation that express a less heroic concept of the ethical subject that is truer to the picture of ethical subjectivity that I want to advance? More specifically still, might not *humour* be one of those forms? The picture of human finitude that I would like to propose is better approached as *comic acknowledgement* rather than tragic affirmation. This is an acknowledgement of both the ubiquity of the finite and its ungraspability. My approval of the demand of finitude is not equal to that demand, but makes that demand all the more demanding. There is no way that I can freely assume the necessity of the ethical demand like Schelling's Oedipus. Its radically one-sided unfulfillability sunders my ethical subjectivity in a manner that entails the endless inadequacy of my action. As such, any foaming wave of authenticity slips away into a deeper undertow of inauthenticity. My global claim is that humour is a prime expression of this inauthenticity. Humour is a more minimal, less heroic form of sublimation that allows the subject to bear the excessive, indeed hyperbolic, burden of the ethical demand without that demand turning into obsessive self-hatred and cruelty. Paradoxically, one might say that the problem with the tragic-heroic paradigm is that because of its implicit claim to authenticity it is not tragic enough and that humour is more tragic than tragedy because it perpetually forestalls the possibility of authenticity.[20]

Unlike Heidegger, whose work bewilders for its almost entirely uniform humorlessness, Lacan is not without much surrealistic brio and comic *élan*, and his texts abound in puns, conceits, jokes and even occasional references to the Marx Brothers; he even manages the sublime feat of saying both fascinating and witty things about Joyce's *Finnegans Wake*. But my basic intuition here is Freudian rather than Lacanian and it is found not in the well-known 1905 *Jokes and Their Relation to the Unconscious*, but in his brilliant, brief but too little-known late essay called 'Humour' from 1927.[21] In the space of a few pages, and with the telegraphic conciseness of his late style, Freud shows how the phenomenon of humour is the contribution made to the comic by the super-ego. Recall that the thesis of the 1905 Jokebook is that jokes are the contribution of the unconscious to the comic. In humour, the super-ego observes the ego from an inflated position, which makes the ego itself look tiny and trivial. The core insight of the paper is that in humour I find myself ridiculous and I acknowledge this in laughter or simply in a smile. Humour is essentially self-mocking ridicule.

As always when he is at his best, Freud is detained and perplexed by an empirical item, in this case a joke, a case of what André Breton would call at the end of the 1930s, directly inspired by the 1927 paper, *l'humour noir*. In a real sense, all Freudian humour – indeed, all humour – is replete with the unhappy black bile, the *melan-cholia*. Freud speaks of a criminal who, on the morning of his execution, is being led out to the gallows to be hanged, and who remarks, looking up at the sky, '*Na, die Woche fängt gut an*', 'Well, the week's beginning nicely.'[22] Freud asks himself: why is this funny? How is this funny? In the terminology of the later Freud, the humour here is generated by the super-ego observing the ego, which produces *un humour noir* that is not depressing but rather liberating and elevating. Freud's precise words are '*befreiend, erhebend*'. He concludes the little essay on humour with the following words, 'Look! Here is the world, which seems so dangerous! It is nothing but a game for children, just worth making a jest about.'[23]

But why is this important? In my view, the key insight that inaugurates the originality of Freud's later work, what is usually called the Second Topography, is the *splitting of the ego*. This takes places in Freud's analyses of narcissism and melancholy. In the classic 1915 essay, 'Mourning and Melancholia', Freud asks: if mourning is the response to the death of the beloved – what he rather cruelly calls 'object-loss' – then to what is melancholy a response given that no one has died, that is, there was no object to lose?[24] This perplexity is resolved by the fact that in melancholy the ego itself becomes an object. What this means is that there is a splitting of the ego between itself and a critical agency that observes it. This agency is what Freud will later call the *Über-Ich*, the 'over-I' or 'super-ego' that stands over against the ego, critically denigrating it. In the 1915 essay, Freud simply calls it *conscience, das Gewissen*. The originality of the phenomenon of melancholy is that once the investment or 'cathexis' in the object has been withdrawn, then the poles of subject and object are interior to the ego, or rather they are poles of a splitting in the ego where the latter itself becomes the object that is hated and treated sadistically. At this point, my self-insight and self-criticism can turn into the much nastier phenomena of self-hatred, and self-punishment. Let's take the examples of anorexia and suicide. In the former, there is an obvious and painful splitting between the actual body and the body-image, where the anorexic looks in the mirror and insists that they are still too fat while they may well be at the point of collapsing through starvation. Similarly, but even more painfully, the Freudian explanation of suicide is not that I kill myself, but rather than I kill the hated other that I have become; it is *that* detestable thing whose existence I want to end.

The escape from the self-hatred of melancholia lies in its counter-concept, *mania*. Freud writes, 'The most remarkable characteristic of melancholia . . . is its tendency to change around into mania.'[25] Here we have a classic example of what Freud describes in his essay on the drives as an instinctual vicissitude, where something reverses into its opposite, the way love can flip over into hate, sadism into masochism, voyeurism into exhibitionism.[26] As such, mania is the same as melancholia insofar as they are opposed manifestations of the same complex, the only difference being that in melancholy the ego succumbs to the complex, whereas in mania it pushes it aside – in my depression, my mood may suddenly swing around into elation, levity and a sense of triumph. Freud insists that manic states such as joy, exaltation and triumph depend on the same psychical energy as melancholia. The point here is that melancholia and mania are two ends of the same piece of string, and the relation between them is powerfully ambivalent.

In the paper on humour, looking over his shoulder to the arguments of 'Mourning and Melancholia', Freud writes of 'The alternation between melancholia and mania, between a cruel suppression of the ego by the super-ego and a liberation of the ego after that pressure . . .'.[27] And it is here that the originality of the paper on humour can be seen, for Freud's remarks on humour show that the splitting of the ego does not only produce the alternating pathologies of melancholia and mania, with their endless to and fro, but also produces humour – dark, sardonic, wicked humour. In addition to the self-laceration of depression and the self-forgetfulness of elation there is a (decidedly non-Blairite) third way, namely humour. Humour has the same formal structure as depression, but it is an anti-depressant that works by the ego finding itself ridiculous. The subject looks at itself like an abject object and instead of weeping bitter tears, it laughs at itself and finds consolation therein. Humour is an anti-depressant that does not work by deadening the ego in some sort of Prozac-induced daze, or by deluding the subject with some transitory experience of manic joy, but is rather a relation of self-knowledge. Humour is often dark, but always lucid. As Beckett writes in *Watt*:

> The bitter, the hollow and – haw! haw! – the mirthless. The bitter laugh laughs at that which is not good, it is the ethical laugh. The hollow laugh laughs at that which is not true, it is the intellectual laugh. Not good! Not true! Well, well. But the mirthless laugh is the dianoetic laugh, down the snout – haw! – so. It is the laugh of laughs, the *risus purus*, the laugh laughing at the laugh, the beholding, the saluting of the highest joke, in a word the laugh that laughs – silence please – at that which is unhappy.[28]

The pure laugh, the *risus purus*, is the laugh that laughs at the laugh, the laugh that laughs at that which is unhappy. In the absence of Aristotelian happiness, in a world where happiness has been reduced to the maximal satisfaction of transient inclinations, it is in practices like humour that we find an experience of non-delusory, non-desultory and non-heroic sublimation.

I would argue that humour recalls us to the modesty and limitedness of the human condition, a limitedness that calls not for tragic-heroic affirmation but comic *acknowledgement*, not Promethean authenticity but laughable inauthenticity. The anti-depressant of humour works by finding an alternative, positive function for the super-ego, and it is this thought that I would like to explore.

We still have a great deal to learn about the nature of the super-ego

Some versions of psychoanalysis, particularly Lacan's, have a problem with the super-ego. This is not surprising as it is the super-ego that generates the hostility towards the ego that crystal-lizes into the symptom. Thus, in a very real sense, the super-ego is the cause of suffering in the subject. It is the position of the lacerating super-ego that the analyst has to occupy if the analysis is going to proceed with any success. Thus, the patient has to substitute the destructive relation towards the super-ego with a positive transference towards the analyst in order to break down the symptom and attenuate or transform the suffering (*nota bene:* I did not say 'end the suffering'). In psychoanalysis, the hateful watchful presence of the super-ego is exchanged for the more benign and trusted presence of the analyst.

In the penultimate paragraph of the paper on humour, Freud acknowledges that 'In other connections we knew the super-ego as a severe master.' However – and this is what is so interesting about the 1927 paper – what is evinced or glimpsed in humour is a non-hostile super-ego, a super-ego that has undergone what we might call 'maturation', a maturity that comes from learning to laugh at oneself, from finding oneself ridiculous. We might say that in humour the childlike super-ego that experiences parental prohibi-tion and Oedipal guilt is replaced with a more grown up super-ego, let's imaginatively call it 'super-ego II'. Freud writes in the final paragraph of the 1927 paper, 'If it is really the super-ego which, in humour, speaks such kindly words of comfort to the intimidated ego, this will teach us that we still have a great deal to learn about the nature of the super-ego.'[29] True enough, Freud and his commentators have said many inconsistent things about the super-ego. My point, however, is simple: in humour, we see the profile of 'super-ego II', a super-ego which does not lacerate the ego, but speaks to it words of unsentimental consolation. This is a positive super-ego that liberates and elevates by allowing the ego to find itself ridiculous. If 'super-ego I' is the prohibiting parent, scolding the child, then 'super-ego II' is the comforting parent. Or better still, 'super-ego II' is the child that has become the parent: wiser, wittier and slightly wizened. It is the super-ego that saves the human being from tragic hubris, from the Promethean fantasy of believing oneself omnipotent, autarkic and authentic, and it does this through humour.

I think that 'super-ego II' finds something of an anticipation in the fascinating reformulation of the super-ego in Loewald's work. In his 1962 paper, 'Super-ego and Time', Loewald basically attempts to think together the categories of Freud's picture of the psychic agencies (ego, super-ego and id) with Heidegger's modes of temporality, where the super-ego is futural, the id is the past and the ego is the present.[30] On this interpretation, the super-ego functions from the standpoint of a future ego that is ahead of the ego and which the ego cannot reach. Perhaps this illuminates the experience of failure or abandonment that the ego might feel with respect to the super-ego. In Heideggerean terms, the super-ego is being-ahead-of-itself and Loewald says that conscience speaks to us from the viewpoint of an inner future that stands ahead of us and whose distance from us we cannot make up. As Goethe counsels: 'what thou hast inherited from thy fathers, acquire it to make it thine'. But this is an endless task. The super-ego is an unfinished task, the work of a future that we cannot quite achieve, the place of an organization of the future before which we always stand somewhat disorganized from the standpoint of the ego. On Loewald's picture, the superego represents a future state of perfection that can never be attained, which leaves us in a state of imperfection, self-division or what I called above originary inauthenticity. The super-ego is that experience of an unattainable future, a perfectibility that I can never bring to perfection. Yet, crucially, in forbidding any achievement of authenticity, such an experience does not paralyse the ego, but rather drives the ethical activity of the subject.[31]

Having a conscience

What I hope to have shown in this chapter is that the model of ethical subjectivity that was proposed in Chapter 2 does not lead to an elaborate variety of self-hatred, where the sheer exorbitance of the ethical demand flips over into an oppressive psychical cruelty. A model of sublimation, largely borrowed from Lacan, allows the subject contact with the source of the ethical demand in a way that does not crush it. Sublimation traces the profile of something sublime: the ethical Thing that is at the heart of the aesthetic object. The transgressions of aesthetic experience both open onto ethical separation and allow for reparation.

We saw how, for Lacan, the privileged mode of sublimation is tragedy and I tried to show how this choice of tragedy is far from random, but places Lacan within the tradition of the philosophy of the tragic that extends back through Heidegger to Schelling. The problem with tragedy is that it risks distorting the picture of finitude by making the subject heroic, by seeing tragic action as a conflict between freedom and necessity that culminates in authenticity or autarchy. Against this, and precisely in order to retain the tragic dimension of ethical experience – as Woody Allen says, 'comedy is tragedy plus time' – an alternative mode of sublimation was presented, namely humour. It was argued that humour is a more minimal and less heroic form of sublimation that is truer to the picture of ethical experience advanced in this book. It might also be added that the genius of humour is the fact that it is a practice, an actually existing and thoroughly everyday practice, where ethical experience is both staged and assuaged.

At this point, we turned to Freud's theory of humour and in particular the novel account of the super-ego at its heart. The essence of humour, for Freud, is self-mocking ridicule, where I look at myself from outside myself and find myself laughably inauthentic. In this way, I hope to have shown that the split at the heart of the ethical subject is not some form of masochistic self-flagellation, but rather *the experience of an ever-divided humorous self-relation*. In this way, I can bear the radicality of the ethical demand because I can laugh at myself. I find myself ridiculous, which is to say that I do not find my *self*, whatever that might mean, but rather see myself from outside and smile. Such is Beckett's *risus purus*.

Humour is, then, the experience of the essential lack of self-coincidence. That is to say, humour is a powerful example of what we might call the human being's *eccentricity* with regard to itself. Perhaps the most fundamental feature of what it means to be human is the fact that we do not coincide with ourselves, the material body that I *am* is not the same as the experience of thinking that I *have*. That is, there is an experiential gap between being and having, between the being that one is and having a relation to that being. More plainly stated, the human being has a reflective attitude towards its experiences and towards itself. This is why human beings are eccentric, because they live beyond the limits set for them by nature by taking up a distance from their immediate experience. In living outside itself in its reflective activity, the human being achieves a break with nature. The philosophical anthropologist Helmuth Plessner goes further and claims that the human *is* this break, this gap between being and having, between the physical and the psychical. The working out of the consequences of the eccentric position of the human is the main task of a philosophical anthropology, which is why laughter has such an absolutely central place in Plessner's work.[32]

We are restless, curious, often disquieted creatures. Pascal would go further and call us wretched, where the human condition is defined for him as 'inconstancy, boredom and anxiety'. However, the self-consciousness of our wretchedness is also, for Pascal, the condition of possibility for recognizing our greatness, a greatness that flows from our wretchedness. This is the great virtue of the comic: if there is a black sun of melancholia at the heart of the comic universe, then this does not imply depression. On the contrary, with the anti-depressant of humour we can laugh at ourselves and find not sadness, but what Freud called 'liberation and elevation', a lucid consolation.

Let me go back to the word that I passed over too quickly in my discussion of Freud: *conscience*. The internalization of the ethical demand that splits open the subject between itself and a demand that it cannot meet is nothing other than the experience of conscience. As I mentioned in the Introduction, Luther defines conscience as the work of God in the heart of man. In having a conscience, God is inside you, an ever-watchful presence with no mediation through shamans or priests. One needn't be a Feuerbachian to want to replace the idea of conscience as the work of God with the idea that conscience is the work of the human being upon itself, even if the demand that we might make upon ourselves is, as we saw with Løgstrup, to be God-like. Conscience is not the work of God within us, but the work of ourselves upon ourselves. This work on the self can be excessively demanding work. On my account, conscience is the location of the ethical demand, a demand that is impossibly demanding, a demand to be infinitely responsible, a demand that divides us, that sunders us. It is indeed true, as Nietzsche would claim, that without the experience of sublimation, conscience cruelly vivisects the subject, it pulls us apart. This is why we require the less heroic but possibly more tragic form of sublimation that I have tried to describe in this chapter. The question to be posed now is the following: what is the relation, if any, between the model of ethical subjectivity that I have developed and political action? More precisely yet, what is the relation between the experience of conscience and politics?

4

Anarchic metapolitics – political subjectivity and political action after Marx

The decisive element in every situation is the permanently organized and long prepared force which can be put into the field when it is judged that a situation is favourable (and it can be favourable only insofar as such a force exists, and is full of fighting spirit). Therefore, the essential task is that of systematically and patiently ensuring that this force is formed, developed and rendered ever more homogenous, compact, and self-aware.

Antonio Gramsci

I began this book by claiming that philosophy begins in disappointment, both religious and political. The massive political disappointment or drift of the present can be felt in numerous ways, but essentially disappointment is the response to a situated injustice or wrong that provokes the need for an ethics. The hope is that such an ethics might be able to face and face down the iniquities of the present. This led to the meta-ethical argument for ethical experience and ethical subjectivity outlined in Chapter 1, based in the concepts of approval and demand, where an ethical subject was conceived as the way in which the self binds itself willingly to some conception of the good. This meta-ethical argument was illustrated with the example of Kant and the problem of the fact of reason in his work and that of certain contemporary neo-Kantians. An 'autonomy orthodoxy' in ethics was identified, and the heterodox counter-possibility of an alternative approach was sketched, where ethics is based on what I called the 'hetero-affectivity' of the other's demand. This was pursued at length in the more normative argument of Chapter 2 with the examples of Badiou, Løgstrup, Levinas and Lacan. I attempted to construct a model of ethical subjectivity based on the idea of fidelity or commitment to an ethical demand that is one-sided, radical and unfulfillable. This demand hetero-affectively divides subjectivity between itself and a demand that cannot be fulfilled. Namely, that the demand whose approval makes me the ethical subject that I am, ends up dividing me from myself. In the preceding chapter, I pursued this thought in relation to the experience of conscience and an alternative picture of the super-ego where I look at myself from outside myself and find myself ridiculous – 'well, the week's beginning nicely'. Although the main target of the last chapter was the objection that my model of ethical subjectivity leads to a form of self-lacerating masochism, what hopefully became clear in its closing pages was the way in which the infinitely demanding ethics of commitment can be sublimated into the humorous self-division of the ethical subject. Such a demanding ethics 'dividuates' us from ourselves humorously and humanly, showing the eccentricity of the human being with respect to itself. It is in our endless inauthenticity, failure and lack of self-mastery that our ethical dignity consists.

This brings us to the final step in the argument, the passage from ethics to politics, or, more precisely, from an ethics of infinitely demanding commitment to a politics of resistance. This is the ambition of the present chapter. A clue to the shape of this politics was noted in passing in the Introduction when I talked about political disappointment in relation to the motivational deficit in the institutions of liberal democracy, a deficit that is also moral. What is required, I argued, is a conception of ethics that begins by acknowledging this motivational deficit, but without accepting the potent temptations of either active or passive nihilism: Buddhistic passivity or Jihadist or Christian fundamentalist activism. Yet, I also claimed that this motivational deficit with regard to liberal democracy has had positive effects. Namely, that the dissatisfaction of citizens with traditional electoral forms of politics and institutions has led to an explosion of non-electoral engagement and activism, such as the movements critical of neo-liberal globalization, indigenous rights groups, NGOs and various networked groups of activists, some of which will be examined below. As such, the demotivating effects of liberal democracy can also be politically remotivating. The wider purpose of this book is to provide an ethical orientation that might support this remotivation. The purpose of this final chapter is to provide an argument that is both descriptive and normative as to how such a politics might be conceived. That is, it is both a description of what might be said to be happening in contemporary activist politics and a recommendation as to how that activism might begin to conceive of itself in the future. The ethical energy for the remotivation of politics and democracy can be found in those plural, dispersed and situated anti-authoritarian groups that attempt to articulate the possibility of what I will call below, with Marx, 'true democracy'.

However, in order to get to the point where I can attempt to weld together ethics and politics, an account of what is meant by politics must be given. To do this, for reasons that I hope soon become clear, I would like to turn to Marx. As the argument of this chapter moves through a number of distinct moments, let me try and lay it out in some detail. I begin by trying to identify what I see as the truth of Marx's work, namely his description of the emergence and nature of capitalism through the hegemony of the bourgeoisie and the reduction of socio-economic life to the circulation of commodities through the universal equivalent of money. However, I then go on to dispute what Marx saw as the political corollary of this socio-economic analysis, namely the simplification of class positions into one basic antagonism (bourgeoisie/proletariat) and the emergence of the proletariat as the revolutionary class who would be the agent for the emancipation of humanity. Against Marx, I argue that the accelerating dislocatory power of capitalism does not lead to the emergence of a unique political subject, but rather to the multiplication of social actors, defined in terms of locality, language, ethnicity, sexuality or whatever. As such, the task after Marx is the reactivation of politics through the articulation of new political subjectivities. It is at this point that I borrow Gramsci's idea of hegemony, understood as the formation of collective will and political associations out of the divergent groupings that make up civil society and which is based in local and situated forms of commonality. The political task of subject formation, then, cannot be articulated in relation to a pregiven socio-economic identity like that of the proletarian, but has to be invented or aggregated from the various social struggles of the present. The problem of political subjectivity is a question of *naming*, of naming a political subject and organizing politically around that name. That is, the logic of political nomination consists in identifying a determinate particularity in society and then hegemonically constructing that particularity into a generality that exerts a universal claim.

It is at this point that I discuss the examples of struggles for indigenous rights in the Mexican and, to a lesser extent, Australian contexts. The key lesson of these struggles is that indigenous identity is a political achievement and not an accident of birth or an extra-political cultural given. What is fascinating about these examples is the way in which a new political subject arises in a situation, against the repressive activity of the state, through the articulation of a new universal name – the indigenous. I think this reveals a novel political function for rights: they can be levers of political articulation whereby a hitherto marginalized constituency enters into public visibility by raising a universal claim in relation to a situation of injustice or a wrong. Keeping these examples in mind, I then turn to the question of the state. Criticizing the Leninist idea of the withering away of the state, I argue that politics should be conceived at a distance from the state, taking up a distance in a specific situation. More specifically, at a time when the state is seeking to saturate and control more and more areas of social life, I claim that the task of radical political articulations is the creation of *interstitial* distance within the state territory and try and show how this might be said to describe the forms of direct democratic action that have provided the cutting edge to radical politics since the mobilization against the meeting of the WTO in Seattle in 1999.

Politics, then, is praxis in a situation that articulates an inter-stitial distance from the state and allows for the emergence of new political subjects who exert a universal claim. Returning once more to Marx, I try and show how this conception of politics corresponds to what the very young Marx calls 'true democracy' in his critique of Hegel's conception of the state. Turning Hegel on his head (or right side up – it depends how you see it), Marx claims that Hegel mystifies the state and is mistaken in his critique of universal suffrage and popular sovereignty. The key to politics for Marx is the idea of popular self-determination, what the later Marx calls 'an association of free human beings', expressed in the idea of true democracy against the state.

I then return to the ethical arguments of the opening chapters of the book and try and make good the hinge between ethics and politics. I seek to show that political action does not flow from the cunning of reason, some materialist or idealist philosophy of history, or socio-economic determinism, but rather from what I describe as a 'metapolitical' moment of ethical experience of the kind described in this book. Politics is an ethical practice that arises in a situation of injustice which exerts a demand for responsibility. It is at this point that I seek to link my argument to two meanings of *anarchism*, one ethical and the other political. The ethical meaning of anarchism is derived from Levinas and concerns his critique of the 'archic' character of subjectivity in modern philosophy. On Levinas's view, and this recalls the claim I made about the 'autonomy orthodoxy' in chapter 1, it is the sovereign, self-positing subject that has dominated modern philosophy since Descartes, where the *archè* or principle governing selfhood is autarchy, understood as self-origination or self-legislation. Against this, Levinas argues that ethical subjectivity is affected by the other in a way that places in question the self's purported sovereignty and autonomous majesty. In this sense, the ethical relation to the other is anarchical, which, for Levinas, is not devoid of political significance.

Politically, what is most compelling about anarchism is its emphasis on ethics as a binding factor in political practice, as opposed to the silence or hostility to ethics that one finds in Marx and in many Marxist and post-Marxist thinkers. In my view, anarchism – what we might call 'actually existing anarchism' – is a powerfully refreshing and remotivating response to the drift and demotivation of liberal democracy. In particular, and this links back to the arguments about humour in the previous chapter, it is the carnivalesque humour of anarchist groups and their tactics of 'non-violent warfare' that have lead to the creation of a new language of civil disobedience and a recovery of the notion of direct democracy. However, although I will come back to this point below, there is an important difference between the position I argue for and classical anarchism. Classically – and rightly – anarchism was always concerned with freedom and struggles for liberation. If one looks at anarchist texts from the 1960s this concern with freedom was focused on sexual liberation from repressive bourgeois morality. The conception of anarchism that I seek to defend, and which I think is what we find on the ground in activist practice, is not so much organized around freedom as around *responsibility*, an infinite responsibility that arises in relation to a situation of injustice. This is an anarchism of infinite responsibility rather than unlimited freedom, even though the goal of responsible action might be the cultivation of the other's freedom.

It is here, I believe – although this is a moot point – that the implications of Levinas's work for an anarchist politics become compelling.

I conclude with a polemic against traditional philosophical approaches to politics, in Plato and Heidegger say, which I see as essentially anti-political attempts to police the political mani-festation of the people by reducing them to their allotted social function in the totality of the state. Against this tendency, I describe the people as the manifestation of *dissensus* which I want to link to the experience of democracy. On my view, at the core of politics is the anarchic practice of democratic dissensus articulated around an ethical demand that arises in a situation of injustice and inspires the mood of anger, which I see as the first political emotion. In contradistinction to many other theoretical approaches to politics, I do not think that the massive structural dislocations, violences and injustices of the present simply invite pessimism or the arrival of the uncanniest guest of nihilism, whether active or passive. On the contrary, they can also invite militancy and optimism, an occasion for political resistance that arises from the infinite de-mand of an ethical commitment.[1]

Marx's truth

Let me begin by stating what I see as the first truth of Marx's work, namely the analysis of capitalism, an analysis that is truly prophetic and where the economic form of life that began in some rain-soaked corners of north-western Europe, in Holland, England and some of its former colonies has, through processes that we all too easily call globalization, spread its movement of expropriation all across the world. In the opening pages of the *Manifesto of the Communist Party*, Marx and Engels write of the revolutionary role of the bourgeoisie. This shouldn't be forgotten: the bourgeoisie are the outcome of the revolutions of the 1600s in England, the Dutch

Republic, and the somewhat retarded 1789 revolution in France, and they play a revolutionary role in history. As Marx and Engels emphasize, in making profane all that's sacred, in establishing connections, colonies and settlements everywhere, through the power of trade, commerce, colonialism and transport (think of Marx's wonderfully eulogistic remarks on the importance of shipping, railways and canals), the bourgeoisie globalizes itself, becoming *cosmopolitan*. In sharp contrast to the current vogue that the concept of cosmopolitanism enjoys amongst many writers and theorists, Marx sees cosmopolitanism as the *pseudo-internationalism* of atomized individualism that would have to be contrasted with a true international.

In stripping the veneer of naturalness from all social relations, including family relations and the formerly prized professions and hierarchies of feudal society, in making the experience of labour unbearable and indeed crippling through industrial organization, the bourgeoisie reveal the *contingency* of social life and what we might call its *historicity*: the possibility that the particular set of social arrangements through which we are living are the outcome of a transformative social process and are therefore capable of being transformed. Through the extraordinary energy that they expended on the overthrow of feudalism in its various forms, the bourgeoisie unwittingly reveals the *political* character of social life. In reducing those social relations to essentially monetary relations, in creating a world market based on the abstract universality of money and the experience of self-estrangement and alienation, the bourgeoisie is the condition of possibility for anti-bourgeois political struggles. Marx and Engels write in the *Manifesto*:

> Where it has come to power the bourgeoisie has obliterated all relations that were feudal, patriarchal, idyllic. It has pitilessly severed the motley bonds of feudalism that joined men to their natural superiors, and has left intact no other bond between one man and another than naked self-interest, unfeeling "hard

cash". It has drowned the ecstasies of religious fervour, of
zealous chivalry, of philistine sentiment in the icy waters of
egoistic calculation. It has resolved personal worth into exchange value, and in place of countless attested and hard-
won freedoms it has established a single freedom – conscienceless free trade. In a word, for exploitation cloaked by religious
and political illusions, it has substituted unashamed, direct,
brutal exploitation.[2]

Ours is a universe where human relations have been reduced to
naked self-interest, to unfeeling hard cash, and where all social life
is governed by one imperative: conscienceless free-trade; a life of
open, unashamed, direct and brutal exploitation. We inhabit what
Marx would see as an M–C–M (money for commodities for more
money) matrix of the increasingly centralized expropriation of the
vast majority of humanity. In one of the striking scientific metaphors with which Marx begins *Capital*, the commodity is described
as the cell-form in the body of capitalist economy, its basic element
or unit.[3] Money is the universal equivalent by virtue of which
commodities are exchanged, it is the blood that feeds the circu-
latory system of capitalism. If the first volume of *Capital* were
brutally reduced to a formula, then we might offer this: money
circulates commodities.

Reading Marx on the genesis and emergence of capital and its
political corollary, the modern representative state; reading him on
the function of money as the universal, yet alienated, capacity of
humankind; on commodity fetishism and the mystified nature of
exchange value; on the massive structural dislocations of capitalist
society and the yawning inequalities that it produces, one is simply
persuaded of the massive prescience and truth of these analyses.
History has proven Marx more successful than he could possibly
have imagined in his intention, in another of those metaphors from
the beginning of *Capital*, in laying bare the economic law of motion
of modern capitalist society.[4]

Capitalism capitalizes

Sadly, what I have just said is the easy part. For me, Marx's analysis of capitalism remains the *sine qua non* for the understanding of contemporary socio-economic life. However, what follows from this for our thinking about politics? That is the question. Are we witnessing, as Marx and Engels foresaw with particular clarity in the *Manifesto*, a simplification of the class structure into the opposed poles of bourgeoisie and proletariat? Are we witnessing the emergence of a revolutionary class whose seizure of power, whose dictatorship as Lenin insists in *State and Revolution*, entails the withering away of the state and the implementation of socialism? Are the undoubted and massive dislocations of capitalist globalization – and just think about what Marx would have said about what has been happening over the past years in South China or regions of India – producing a classless class, a class who will bring about the overcoming of the division of labour and the achievement of communism? In Marx's famous words at end of the first volume of *Capital*, will the expropriators be expropriated?[5]

Let's just say that I have my doubts. Rather than a simplification of class positions, one might talk of a multiplication of class actors in society, of society being made up by an increasingly complex fabric of class identifications, rendered even more intricate by other sets of identifications, whether gender, ethnicity, sexual orientation or whatever. In such a situation, we cannot hope, as the classical Marxist economism of the Second International maintained, that once the economic laws of motion of capitalist society have been laid bare, then revolution will follow quasi-automatically from the contradictions and crises of the capitalist system. Crisis-ridden as it doubtless is and has been since at least the 1850s, capitalism is wonderfully persistent and can morph into new shapes at the least sign of resistance, brilliantly recuperating anything that seems to place it in question. Since the time of the Situationist International in the 1960s, we have begrudgingly come to admit that *recuperation* is the fate of all forms of avant-gardist revolutionary *détournement*, whether aesthetic or political. So, rather than evolving towards a revolution that would take us beyond it, one might say that *capitalism capitalizes* – it simply produces more capitalism. It makes rather quaint, sad reading to look at accounts of Marx from the 1970s, where figures like Ernest Mandel wrote that 'capitalism's heyday is over'.[6] On the contrary, capitalism under the guise of globalization is spreading its tentacles of expropriation to every corner of the earth. If someone found a way of overcoming capitalism, then some corporation would doubtless buy the copyright and the distribution rights.[7]

In other words, we cannot sit back and hope that the structural contradictions of capitalism will do the job of political transformation on our behalf. We cannot reduce the sphere of the political to the socio-economic, as is suggested by the crude base–superstructure model with which Marx flirted in the 'Preface' to *The Contribution to the Critique of Political Economy* and which became an article of faith for Engels and the Marxism of the Second International.[8] On the contrary, to borrow a term from Husserl's late work, it is a question of reactivating the *political* dimension of Marxism, a dimension that will require all our capacity for political invention and imagination. Since the late 1970s, there is no doubt that it is the right who have been spectacularly more successful than the left in deploying such a political imagination. Whether one thinks of Thatcher, Reagan and the New Right of the 1980s; of the various post-Soviet nationalisms in Russia and its former satellite states; of the multiple and flourishing xenophobic parties and regimes in Continental Europe; of the sheer political tenacity of the Republican campaign against Al Gore and the *coup d'état* in Florida in 2000; of the ideological mobilization of 9/11 into a war against terror which culminated in George W. Bush's re-election in November 2004, where neo-liberal policies were sold as a moral backlash against so-called liberal values to the very blue-collar voters who had nothing to gain and much to lose from neo-liberalism, then there can be little question that it is the right that has best understood the nature of politics in recent history.[9]

To be clear, when I speak about reactivating the political dimension of Marxism, I do not say this in order to embrace what some have called 'disco-Marxism', that is, an approach that abandons the socio-economic dimension by reducing all experience to modes of discourse, a gesture that politicizes Marxism at the price of leaving capitalism unquestioned. On the contrary, I think that the goal of communism as articulated in the *Manifesto*, namely what Marx and Engels call, in a nuanced way, the '*Aufhebung* of private property', that is, both its maintenance *and* its overcoming, but not an abolition, *Abschaffung*, is an entirely legitimate political aspiration.[10] The issue with regard to capitalism is therefore the establishment of capital as a social product and not a personal one, of removing the class-character of private property. But this is also a political task. In this connection, it is helpful to recall Gramsci's concept of 'historical bloc'. Opposing the determination of the superstructure by the base in economistic Marxism, a historical bloc is the unity of base and superstructure. Following Gramsci, a critique of economistic reductionism need not necessarily lead to ignoring the economic dimension but incorporating the latter into a wider ethical-political and ideological strategy; as Gramsci writes, 'For though hegemony is ethico-political, it must also be economic'.[11]

Dislocation

Another way of thinking about what I called the first truth of Marx's work is in terms of the accelerating dislocatory power of capitalism. To assert, as I did, that capitalism capitalizes is to say that it produces more and more extensive and aggravated social and economic dislocations, all over the surface of the earth. This entails increasing demographic movements from the country to the city or from the south to the north, the creation of vast shanty towns of the dislocated poor, the dislocation of local industries and practices by cut-price commodities from overseas and the phenomenon of what is now euphemistically called 'outsourcing'. In his most important programmatic theoretical text – his manifesto, if you will – the title essay from the 1990 book *New Reflections on the Revolution of Our Time*, Ernesto Laclau writes,

> In one sense, our analysis keeps within the field of Marxism and attempts to reinforce what has been one of its virtues: the acceptance of the transformations entailed by capitalism and the construction of an alternative project that is *based on* the ground created by those transformations and not on *opposition* to them. Commodification, bureaucratization, and the increasing dominance of scientific and technological planning over the division of labour should not necessarily be resisted. Rather, one should work within these processes so as to develop the prospects they create for a non-capitalist alternative.[12]

Despite the fact that, for Marx, the dislocations of capitalist society are orientated structurally or systemically by his misguided teleology of a simplification of the class structure and the emergence of a revolutionary subject – the proletariat – this should not obscure the truth of Marx's work, which is its radically unsentimental, unromantic and anti-conservative diagnosis of capitalism. The dislocatory power of capitalism must be affirmed and not resisted by a retreat into some sort of Rousseauesque and ultimately reactionary romantic anti-capitalism. On the contrary, the more dislocated the ground upon which capitalism operates, the less it can rely on a framework of supposedly natural or stable social and political relations. Capitalist dislocation, in its ruthless destruction of the bonds of tradition, local belonging, family and kinship structures that one might have considered natural, reveals the contingency of social life, that is, its constructed character, which is to say, its *political* articulation. This is the moment of what Laclau, after Gramsci, calls *hegemony*. Once the ideological illusions of the natural have been stripped away and revealed as contingent formations by capitalist dislocation, where freedom, for example, becomes the precarious experience of insecurity when one sells oneself on the labour market, then the only cement that holds political identities together is a hegemonic link.

Initially, hegemony means leadership of a class alliance, exemplified in the Russian revolutions of 1905 and 1917, where the proletariat became hegemonic. Yet, this is not an economic or economistic alliance, but the construction of a system of political alliances, what Laclau calls a 'chain of equivalences'. The meaning of hegemony is expanded to include cultural, moral and ideological leadership over allied subordinate groups, the formation of a new ideological terrain, a new space of myth in the sense of Georges Sorel.[13] Such hegemony has to be based on consent, it has to be the cultivation of a *habitus*. Originally, the concept of hegemony derives from linguistics (Gramsci's unfinished university thesis was in linguistics), meaning the influence or prestige of one language over another, for example the increasing hegemony of Spanish over English in the USA. Hegemony is active, dynamic and changing, as opposed to the static model of subordination implied by the model of a dominant ideology. It is the cultivation of the art of government amongst the subaltern classes.

For Gramsci, hegemony is the activity of the formation of 'collective will' out of the divergent groupings that make up civil society, but it is still deeply anchored in the fundamental Marxist dialectical contradiction of forces and relations of production. For Laclau, the concept of hegemony is freed from this contradiction and expanded to designate the general logic of the political institution of the social.[14] The task of hegemony is the cultivation of forms of commonality, of habits, customs and a whole ethos of what Gramsci calls 'common sense'. This is the role that Gramsci assigns to what he calls 'philosophy of praxis', which is both his code in the *Prison Notebooks* for Marxism and a critique of the latter insofar as Marxism should not present itself as an abstract theory, but should enter into and, in turn, shape common sense. Hegemony is the construction of chains of equivalence, of political alliances between often quite disparate groups, based on consent and local, situated forms of commonality.

The ever-widening dislocations of an increasingly brutal and far-reaching capitalism do not, however, entail political pessimism, as is the case for an Adorno or a Heidegger from opposite sides of the philosophical looking-glass. On the contrary, such dislocations *can* (I emphasize 'can' as there is no necessity to this operation and no appeal to any political theodicy or philosophy of history) be linked to the emergence of a range of alternative political possibilities opposed to capitalism and are thus, as Laclau says, the condition for 'a new militancy and a new optimism'.[15] He writes:

> The fragmentation and growing limitation of social actors is linked to the multiplication of the dislocations produced by 'disorganized capitalism'. It follows from this that more and more areas of social life must become the product of *political* forms of reconstruction and regulation.[16]

The radical and perhaps disquieting thought here is for a co-implication of the dislocatory force of capitalist globalization, a multiplication of social actors and, thus, of political possibility. This co-implication *can* lead to the emergence of an alternative left, but this is a hegemonic operation, it is a construction, it is political work that needs to be done. All of which has significant implications for our thinking of the *subject* of politics, as we will now see.

The names are lacking –
the problem of political subjectivity

Politics is always about nomination. It is about naming a political subjectivity and organizing politically around that name. Marx's name for the political subject is the proletarian, more specifically the proletarian as communist. Can this be our name? Are we united around the fact of our proletarian identity? I do not think so. Despite the sociological fact that the industrial working-class no longer plays an obviously hegemonic role in revolutionary politics, the reasons for doubting Marx's position would take us deep into a critique of Marx's ontology. By ontology I mean Marx's conception of the being of being human, which is expressed in a cluster of related concepts: the idea of species-being (*Gattungswesen*), being as production, being as praxis, or being as the practical self-activity of the subject. As I tried to show in Chapter 1, these are ideas that Marx owes to the 'autonomy orthodoxy' of Kant, Fichte and Hegel, a tradition that Marx both completes and completely overturns. As already suggested, if Hegel can be said to socialize the purported solipsism of Kantian or Fichtean autonomy, locating it in relations of intersubjectivity, then Marx can be said to communize autonomy locating it in the activity and life-praxis of the proletariat. The point here is that, for Marx, communism is an ontological category before it is that around which any political activism can orientate itself, and it is the link between ontological and political activity that allows Marx to claim that the proletariat are the classless class who incarnate the emancipatory interests of humanity. To put it bluntly, I think that the category of the proletarian as revolutionary subject has decisively broken down sociologically and is hostage to a highly dubious ontology. Therefore, we lack a name around which a radical politics can take shape.

The political task, then, is one of inventing a name around which a political subject can be aggregated from the various social struggles through which we are living. This act of the aggregation of the political subject is the moment of hegemony. More accurately still, following through on the thought of the multiplication of social actors in the contemporary world, it is perhaps a question of inventing situated *names* for that around which politics can hegemonize itself and then aggregating those names into some sort of association, common front or collective will. The logic of political nomination, I take it, is that a determinate particularity in society is hegemonically constructed into a universality. This is what Laclau calls 'hegemonic universality'. That is, the universal is not read off from the script of some pre-given ontology but posited in a specific situation. Universality is constructed in a specific context in relation to what Gramsci calls common sense. Marx gets close to this thought in an unnervingly contemporary sentence from his 1843 'Introduction' to the *Critique of Hegel's Philosophy of Right*, where the logic of the political subject is expressed in the words: '*I am nothing and I should be everything*' ('*Ich bin nichts, und ich müßte alles sein*').[17] That is, beginning from a position of emptiness, a particular group posits the fullness of the universal and hegemonically articulates that universality in political action, thereby becoming a political subject.[18]

Although they are old names, some people assert that immigrant, asylum seeker, or refugee could be candidates for political names.[19] Others think that 'multitude' in the sense of Michael Hardt and Antonio Negri is a new political name. This is clearly the implicit ambition of the powerful analysis of the emergent form of network sovereignty given in the hugely influential *Empire* from 2000, an ambition made explicit in the 2004 sequel, *Multitude*, which argues that the multitude is the new political subject and political alternative that grows within empire.[20] Yet, I would dispute this view both because the analysis given in *Empire* at the ontological level risks retreating into the very anti-dialectical materialist ontology of substance that Marx rightly criticized in his early work and also because it makes the work of politics too systemic insofar as both empire and multitude, that is, both capitalism and the resistance to capitalism, originate in the same ontological substance. It is rather rare for books to be refuted empirically, but I think this happened to *Empire* on September 11th, 2001.[21] More generally, if we are doing politics, we cannot and should not pin our hopes on any ontology, whether a Marxian notion of species-being, a Spinozo-Deleuzianism of abundance, a Heideggero-Lacanianism of lack, or any version of what Stephen White has called 'weak ontology' in politics.[22] On my view, politics is a disruption of the ontological domain and separate categories are required for its analysis and practice. There is no transitivity between ontology and politics.

One needs to search for the struggle

On the topic of the construction of political subjectivity, I would like to illustrate my argument with an example borrowed from the research of Courtney Jung.[23] She is trying to develop what she calls a 'critical liberalism'; although in my view – and I count this as a virtue – it is more critical than liberal. The topic of this far-reaching work is the nature of indigenous political identity in the Mexican context. More specifically, it concerns the emergence of indigenous identity as a political category. Jung's argument is that indigenous identity is a political achievement and not an accident of birth or a given of some supposedly extra-political sphere of culture. On her view, the problem with contemporary liberal political theorists, from Rawls onwards, is that they interpret a phenomenon like indigenous identity as a trans-historical, extra-political, psycho-social given that some-how has to be accommodated in the democratic space of the liberal polity. Against this position, Jung advances three claims:

> First, I argue that identities like peasant and indigenous are a political achievement and not an accident of birth. Second,

the state is not super-imposed on a society already divided among competing and incompatible world-views. The state itself plays a crucial role in transforming distinct practices and traditions into social categories. Third, such potential categories are transformed into identities by the existence of a discourse of rights that establishes an implicit promise. Activists exploit the gap opened by such a promise to shape an identity that can sustain a legitimate claim on the state, that is, a claim the state will hear, and that others in the general public will recognize.

Rather than engage in the usual philosophical business of normative theorizing, Jung justifies her claims through the example of Mexican political history. After the election of Carlos Salinas de Gortari in 1988 under the shadow of the economic crisis that had forced Mexico to turn to the IMF for aid, the Mexican government began to introduce strict neo-liberal economic reforms. Amongst the measures introduced by Salinas was a reversal of the pro-peasant initiatives of the previous decades, cracking down on peasant organizations, and repressing, incarcerating, intimidating and killing hundreds of peasant activists, all of which obviously led to a sharp decline in peasant activism. Thus, the name 'peasant' ceased to have any purchase, it ceased to grant a voice and be effective. Jung continues.

It is in this space, in which the peasant is disarticulated by the neo-liberal policy turn of the Mexican government, that activists forged an indigenous political identity that would re-establish the condition of rural political agency. It is the existence of International Labor Organization Convention 169, which establishes the collective rights of indigenous people in international law that acts as the condition of an indigenous political identity. Ironically, it was Mexico's ratification of the Convention in 1990 that brought it into effect.

The point here is that indigenous political identity is that rare thing, a brand new political phenomenon. Furthermore, its effects have been far from local and it has led to the creation of transnational alliances. Activists meet annually in Geneva at the Working group on Indigenous Populations and in New York at the UN Permanent Forum for Indigenous Issues. More widely still, international networks like People's Global Action that initiated the original call for days of action against the 1999 WTO meetings in Seattle had their origins in the famous International Encounter for Humanity and Against Neoliberalism, which took place in 1996 'knee-deep in the jungle mud of rainy-season Chiapas', as David Graeber charmingly puts it.[24]

What is fascinating about the example of Mexican indigenous political identity is the way in which a new political subject is formed against the repressive actions of the state through the articulation of a new universal name – the indigenous. It is the strategic occupation of the universalistic terrain of international rights and international law that provides the leverage for a local political articulation that has had global effects. Addressing the same problem mentioned above concerning the disappearance of the proletariat as a viable political subject, Jung writes, a little wistfully:

> 'Indigenous' is the new 'proletariat'. Indigenous people sustain a powerful moral critique against neo-liberal globalization because they are constructed as the literal corporeal embodiment of its antithesis. The indigenous is ancient, communal, traditional and moral, able to draw on a wealth of inherited wisdom to operate in organic sympathy with the earth and its natural resources. Globalization on the other hand, is atomising and amoral, leaving in its wake detritus of unemployed labour, depleted resources and degraded environments. Globalization threatens the indigenous idyll. The indigenous person, and in particular the indigenous woman, stands as a reproach to the

ambition of neo-liberal globalization; she is the emancipatory subject of our time.

However sincerely felt such sentiments might be, in my view it is crucial to grasp the strategic *political* operation behind this new emancipatory subject and not risk naturalizing indigenousness through an appeal to categories like 'ancient, communal, traditional' or notions like 'organic sympathy'. The indigenous person is a political name constructed through a hegemonic operation, she is a contingently articulated subject made possible at a determinate and transient historical point and making possible an intervention and a new and dynamic political sequence. That is not to say that indigenous people are a mere fiction and that the wrongs that have been perpetrated against them are not real. The indigenous person can legitimately make a claim on the state that marginalizes them and owes them redress, but the political point concerns the way in which that claim is to be made through hegemonic invention and imagination. In the words of Luis Hernandez Cruz, a well-known leader of the peasant uprisings in the Chiapas in the 1970s and 1980s, who had become an elected representative, a *diputado*, to the State Congress of Chiapas, '*la lucha hay que buscarla*', 'one needs to search for the struggle'.

I would like to discuss another example of indigenous political struggle, this time from Australia.[25] In 1972, in reaction to a speech by William McMahon, prime minister of Australia at the time, denying indigenous land claims and continuing mining activities on land sacred to the Aborigines, four activists – Billy Craigie, Tony Coorie, Michael Anderson and Bertie Williams – set up a delegation under a beach umbrella on the lawn facing the National Parliament. The idea was to stay there and protest until indigenous land claims were properly recognized. In an imaginatively theatrical act of political nomination, the umbrella and surrounding tents were baptized the 'Aboriginal Tent Embassy'. As part of the Aboriginal land rights movement, this act had significant consequences. In Oliver Feltham's words,

In 1972, a tent embassy was erected opposite the National Parliament to protest the non-recognition of indigenous land rights. In 1976, a state government – of the Northern Territory – passed the first land rights legislation. In 1992, the High Court of Australia reversed the declaration of *terra nullius* and recognized what they termed 'native title'. However, at the same time the court declared native title inapplicable to any freehold land leading some activists to term the decision the 'biggest landgrab' in the history of colonization. Throughout the 1990s mainstream political debate focused on limiting the consequences of this landmark decision.[26]

In 1788, when the British landed in the place that they named New South Wales with the intention of setting up a penal colony, the land was declared *terra nullius*, uninhabited land belonging to nobody. In this juridico-political act, the 1000 or so settlers – 750 convicts, 211 marines and officers, 21 officers' wives, 32 children and 1 governor – delegitimated and disregarded any claim that the original inhabitants of the land might have had as well as stripping them of their land. It should be remembered that conservative estimates of the population of 'Australia' prior to settlement put the figure at around 300,000, divided into an estimated three to five hundred nations. Many words could be used to describe this situation, but 'uninhabited' is not one of them. In the face of the state's refusal to recognize the illegality of the original act of settlement, indeed the criminality of the act of foundation of what came to be known as 'Australia', Aboriginal activists reflected back to their oppressors their alleged alien status. Using the leverage of a quasi-international embassy, they engaged in a process of political articulation that resulted in placing significant pressure on the state. What we see in this example is how a specific and local intervention in politics – a beach umbrella on a lawn in Canberra – can have the effect of calling into question the entire legality of the state and calling for redress to a massive historical wrong.

These examples can be marshalled into a wider argument about the political function of human rights. Jacques Rancière, to whom we will return below, expresses what he sees as the logic of human rights in the following paradox: 'the rights of man are the rights of those who have not the rights that they have and have the rights that they have not'.[27] This gnomic formula becomes clearer with the example of women's rights in the context of the French Revolution. Namely, that the claim to universality in the Declaration of the Rights of Man and the Citizen concealed an exclusion of women as bearers of those rights. This contradiction was famously pointed out in the statement of Olympe de Gouges that if women are entitled to go to the scaffold, then they are also entitled to go to the assembly. Rancière writes:

> Women could make a two-fold demonstration. They could demonstrate that they were deprived of the rights that they had, thanks to the Declaration of Rights. And they could demonstrate, through their public action, that they had the rights that the Constitution denied to them, that they could enact those rights. So they could act as subjects of the Rights of Man in the precise sense that I mentioned. They acted as subjects that had not the rights that they had and had the rights that they had not.[28]

Women are the excluded supplement to the order of the state that articulate a new political subjectivity by calling into question that order in terms of its own legitimating logic, namely the universality of rights. Women are the uncounted excess to the order of the state that demand to be taken into account and counted through the mechanism of the vote. As such, the political rights of women are a powerful example of politics as the conflictual questioning of consensus and the opening of a space of *dissensus*, to which we will return below. It is this space of dissensus that best expresses the event of politics, an event that the state order always wishes to shut down.

Linking this example together with that of indigenous rights, we might say that rights can be *levers* of political articulation whereby a hitherto invisible or excluded constituency enters into visibility in relation to an injustice or wrong that shows a contradiction in the logic of the state structure. Rights, therefore, can be viewed as levers for hegemonic articulation in a political process whose ethical motivation is a situation of injustice.

Politics as interstitial distance within the state

Keeping these examples of the political function of rights in mind, I would like to move on to the question of the state. We inhabit states. The state – whether national like Britain or France, a supranational quasi-state like the EU, or imperial like the USA – is the framework within which conventional politics takes place. Now, it is arguable that the state is a limitation on human existence and we would be better off without it. It is arguable that without state systems of government, bureaucracy, the police and the military, human beings would be able to cooperate with each other on the basis of free agreement and not merely through obedience to law. It is arguable that interwoven networks of such cooperative associations might begin to cover all fields of human activity so as to substitute themselves for the state. It is arguable that the vertical hierarchy of the state structure could be replaced with horizontally allied associations of free, self-determining human beings. Such is, of course, the eternal temptation of the anarchist tradition, particularly for someone like Kropotkin, and I will come back to anarchism in more detail below.

However – to put it at its most understated – it seems to me that we cannot hope, at this point in history, to attain a complete withering away of the state, either through concerted anarcho-syndicalist or anarcho-communist action or through revolutionary proletarian praxis with the agency of the party. Within classical Marxism, state, revolution and class form a coherent set: there is a revolutionary class, the universal or classless class of the proletariat whose communist politics entails the overthrow of the bourgeois state. The *locus classicus* for this position is Lenin's *State and Revolution*, a text that is, in my view, fatally sundered by conflicting author-itarian and anarchist tendencies. On the one hand, in the name of the 'authentic' Marx, Lenin claims that the bourgeois state must be smashed and replaced by a democratically centralist workers' state – the dictatorship of the proletariat – but, on the other hand, he claims that this is only a pre-condition for the eventual withering away of the state in communism or what he calls the 'fullest democracy'.[29] The condition of possibility for the Leninist with-ering away of the state is the emergence of a revolutionary class, the proletariat, whom Hardt and Negri seek to update into the multitude.[30] Now, if class positions are not simplifying, but on the contrary becoming more complex through the processes of social dislocation described in this chapter, if the revolution is no longer conceivable in a Marxist-Leninist manner, then that means that, for good or ill – let's say for ill – we are stuck with the state. The question then becomes: what should our political strategy be with regard to the state, to the state and states that we're in?

In a period when the revolutionary proletarian subject has decidedly broken down, and along with it the political project of a withering away of the state, I think that politics should be conceived at a *distance* from the state.[31] Or, better, politics is the praxis of taking up distance with regard to the state, working independently of the state, working in a situation. Politics is praxis in a situation and the labour of politics is the construction of new political subjectivities, new political aggregations in specific local-ities, a new dissensual *habitus* rooted in common sense and the consent of those who dissent. In addition to the examples of the politics of indigenous rights discussed above, this is arguably a description of the sort of direct democratic action that has provided the cutting edge and momentum to radical politics since the days of action against the meeting of the WTO in Seattle in 1999 and subsequently at Prague, Nice, Genoa, Quito, Cancun and elsewhere.[32] In the face of the massive re-territorialization of state power in the West after 9/11, this movement has continued in the huge mobilizations against US and UK intervention in Iraq, and in numerous other protests, such as the opposition to the Republican National Convention in New York in late summer 2004. Despite obvious electoral failures, it is the experience of such mobilizations that provides, in my view, the ethical energy for a remotivation of politics and future democratic organization.

However, to forestall a possible misunderstanding, this distance from the state is *within* the state, that is, within and upon the state's territory. It is, we might say, an *interstitial* distance, an internal distance that has to be opened from the inside. What I mean, seemingly paradoxically, is that there *is* no distance within the state. In the time of the purported 'war on terror', and in the name of 'security', state sovereignty is attempting to saturate the entirety of social life. The constant ideological mobilization of the threat of external attack has permitted the curtailments of traditional civil liberties in the name of internal political order, so-called 'homeland security', where order and security have become identified. Such is the politics of fear, where the political might be defined with Carl Schmitt as that activity which assures the internal order of a political unit like a state through the more or less fantastic threat of the enemy.[33] Against this, the task of radical political articulations is the *creation* of interstitial distance within the state territory. The Mexican example of indigenous identity discussed above is a powerful instance of the creation of such a distance, an act of political leverage where the invocation of an international legal convention created the space for the emergence of a new political subject. Similarly, political activism around the so-called illegal immigrants in Paris, the *sans-papiers*, is the attempt to create an interstitial distance whose political demand – 'if one works in France, one is French' – invokes the principle of equality at the basis of the French republic. One works within the state against the state in a political articulation that attempts to open a space of opposition.

Perhaps it is at this intensely situational, indeed local level that the atomizing, expropriating force of neo-liberal globalization is to be met, contested and resisted. That is, resistance begins by occupying and controlling the terrain upon which one stands, where one lives, works, acts and thinks. This needn't involve millions of people. It needn't even involve thousands. It could involve just a few at first. Resistance can be intimate and can begin in small affinity groups. The art of politics consists in weaving such cells of resistance together into a common front, a shared political subjectivity. What is going to allow for the formation of such a political subjectivity – the hegemonic glue, if you will – is an appeal to universality, whether the demand for political representation, equality of treatment or whatever. It is the hope, indeed the wager, of this book that the ethical demand described above – the infinite responsibility that both constitutes and divides my subjectivity – might allow that hegemonic glue to set into the compact, self-aware, fighting force that motivates the subject into the political action spoken of in the epigraph to this chapter.

True democracy

Politics is praxis in a situation that articulates an interstitial distance from the state, and which allows for the emergence of new political subjectivities. Returning to Marx, I would now like to argue that this distance from the state is democratic.

By democracy I therefore do not mean the state-form, in the sense of liberal or constitutional democracy, nor do I mean democracy in the mouth of neo-imperialists where it is no more than a fetish in a legitimating discourse of capitalist expropriation and the *Realpolitik* of war. By contrast, I mean democracy as a movement of democratization that is – dialectically expressed – the truth of the state, a truth that no state incarnates. As I hear it, this talk of democracy as democratization picks up on a strand of the young Marx's thinking that can be found in his 1843 critique of Hegel's *Rechtsphilosophie*, written when Marx was just 25 years old. In these extensive notes, first published in 1927, Marx tries to conceptualize what he calls 'true democracy', '*wahre Demokratie*', against the order of the state. By 'truth', Marx clearly does not mean propositional or empirical truth, but rather truth as true *to* democracy, truth in the sense of the German cognate *treu* that I mentioned in connection with Badiou in Chapter 2, fidelity or loyalty to democracy. He writes: 'It is self-evident that all forms of state have democracy as their truth and for that reason are untrue to the extent that they are not democracy.'[34]

Marx claims that democracy is the resolved enigma of all political constitutions, and by democracy what he means is that in true democracy the political state as a formal apparatus operated by the bureaucratic class, who are the universal class in Hegel, disappears (*untergehe*) and what takes its place is a conception of democracy as democratic self-determination, what he calls the *Selbstbestimmung des Volks*, the self-determination of the people. With a word that remains a constant feature in the vocabulary of Marx's critique of Hegel from 1843 to the Preface to *Capital* in 1873, he argues that Hegel 'mystifies' the state. Whereas, for Hegel, the family and civil society are conceived as mere components of the higher actuality of the state, Marx argues that it is precisely the other way round: 'The fact is that the state issues from the mass of human beings existing as members of families and members of civil society.'[35] Hegel therefore mistakes the ideal for the material: the state is not the condition of possibility for the family and civil society, but is conditioned by them. It is the mass, the material *Menge*, which is the active principle in political life. This entails that the activities and functions of the state are reconnected to the lives of individuals; that is to say, not their physical being, as in the crude eighteenth-century materialism that Marx powerfully and persistently rejects, but their political or social being. The materiality of Marx's materialism lies in social practices. It is a materialism of intersubjective praxis, not objective matter; of social life, not biological life. According to Marx, Hegel forgets that

> . . . particular individuality is a human individual and that the activities and functions of the state are human activities. He forgets that the nature of the 'particular person' is not his beard and blood and abstract *physis*, but his *social quality* and that the affairs of the state are nothing but the modes of action and existence of the social qualities of men.[36]

For Hegel, political sovereignty is incarnated in the person of the monarch; 'the monarch is', Marx writes, 'personified sovereignty'.[37] Standing this idea on its head, Marx claims that sovereignty is located in the *mass* of individuals that make up society. In a witty allusion to Hamlet's soliloquy, Marx writes, '*Souveränität des Monarchen oder des Volkes, das ist die question.*'[38] Marx wants to defend the idea of popular sovereignty and universal suffrage against Hegel's rejection of both. Towards the end of the *Philosophy of Right*, Hegel rejects popular sovereignty as 'one of the confused notions based on a *wild* idea of the *people* (*die **wüste** Vorstellung des **Volkes***)' and goes on to claim that the idea of the people is a 'formless mass and no longer a state'.[39] Slightly later, Hegel argues that to accept the idea of universal suffrage is tantamount to putting, 'the *democratic* element *without any rational form* into the organism of the state (*Staatsorganismus*) . . .'.[40] Now, it is precisely this formless mass of the *demos* that Marx wants to claim is the subject of politics, the subject of what, thinking of the later Merleau-Ponty, we might think of as 'wild democracy'. True democracy, in this sense, would be a *deformation* of the organicism of the state in the name of its material principle, the mass of the people, what Marx refers to in a highly suggestive way as 'the striving (*das Streben*) of civil society'.[41]

For Marx, then, the state is an *abstractum*; the people alone are the *concretum*.[42] From here, in a series of extraordinarily rich and speedily formulated texts from 1843 and 1844, this idea of popular democratic self-determination receives the name 'communism', and, as I will make clear presently, I have reservations about that name. But the thought that I want to retain is the idea of true democracy as not being incarnated in the state, but rather enacted – practically, locally, situationally – at a distance from the state. I am trying to think of democracy as a movement of *disincarnation* that works concretely beneath the state's abstraction. It is the material drive of social being that calls the state into question and calls the established order to account, not in order to do away with the state, desirable though that might well be in some utopian sense, but in order to better it or attenuate its malicious effects. True democracy would be the enactment of cooperative alliances, aggregations of conviviality and affinity at the level of society that materially deform the state power that threatens to saturate them.

Thinking about true democracy in this way would be one way of thinking and reactivating the moment of the political within Marxism, that is, within a Marxist heritage that has tended to reduce the political to the socio-economic and superstructure to base. It would be a way of recovering what Miguel Abensour calls, after J.G.A. Pocock, 'the Machiavellian moment' within Marxism, the moment of decision, articulation, reactivation and event.[43]

I think that it is around such a notion of true democracy, as subjective praxis in a situation, that a gathering, an organization, an aggregation, an association can emerge. I am very interested in this figure of 'association' or 'coalition' in Marx, which appears in many texts: in *The German Ideology*, the *Manifesto*, and *The Poverty of Philosophy*, where in the face of the socially atomizing brutality of

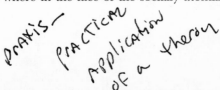

praxis - practical application of a theory

capitalism, Marx understands political organization as what he calls 'the power of united individuals'.[44] This is also what Marx calls in the first volume of *Capital*, '*einen Verein freier Menschen*', 'an association of free human beings'.[45] It is the *ver* that interests me more than the *ein* in this formulation, i.e. the 'one' is that *towards* which we progress without ever constituting the fantasy of what Claude Lefort would call the 'people-as-one', as a unity or fullness. I think such a *Verein* would mean working in common at a certain distance from the state, working towards a control of the place from which one speaks and acts, working together in a situation as a political subject committed to a plan, a place, a space, a process. I think this is not just possible, it is actual, and where it is not actual, it is actualizable: in the interstitial spaces occupied by the dispossessed in the great metropolitan centres, in the shadow zones occupied by refugees and 'illegal' immigrants, or more generally in the workplace, in housing projects, in schools, in universities, in hospitals, in shelters for asylum seekers, all over. True democracy would be the political articulation of these spaces into a common front, a collective will, Gramsci's 'compact and self-aware force'.

However, against Marx, I wouldn't want to call such forms of association communist. The idea of communism remains ontologically suspect because of the essentialist idealist metaphysics of species-being (*Gattungswesen*) that determines the concept in Marx's work. Communism is a word that, in my view, remains captive to an essentially aestheticized and organicist notion of community. This can be traced back to Schiller's *Aesthetic Education of Man* and the 'Oldest System-Programme of German Idealism', attributed to Schelling, Hegel and Hölderlin.[46] It can be traced forward to any number of utterly pernicious social fantasies that Jean-Luc Nancy calls 'immanentism', that is, a conception of social relations based on the fantasy of fusion, unity, fullness and completion. For me, on the contrary, it is a question of trying to conceive of forms of political gathering, coalition or association, that is to say, contingent political articulations in relation to a more wild and formless conception of social being. I would now like to connect these arguments back to the main claim of this book and to two meanings of anarchism, one ethical and the other political.

Ethics as anarchic meta-politics

In my view, what has to be continually criticized in political thinking is the aspiration to a full incarnation of the universal in the particular, or the privileging of a specific particularity because it is believed to *incarnate* the universal: for example, the classical Hegelian idea of the state, the modish and vague idea of a European super-state, or the fantasy of the world-state. By contrast, democracy as democratization is the movement of *disincarnation* that challenges the borders and questions the legitimacy of the state. Democratization is a dissensual praxis that works against the consensual horizon of the state. Democratization is here conceived as a dual sequence of both micro-political articulations, movements and blocs at the level of civil society, and as a sequence of macro-political, trans-national articulations. Good examples of such dual-sequencing would be the politics of indigenous rights and women's rights discussed above and the forms of direct action that took place in Seattle and elsewhere. Circling back to the main argument of this book, the final claim I would like to make is that democratization is action based on an ethical demand. That is to say, political action does not flow from the cunning of reason, from some materialist or idealist philosophy of history or indeed from some more or less secularized eschatology. Rather, it feeds from what I will now describe as a *meta-political* moment.

In my view, at the heart of a radical politics there has to be a meta-political ethical moment. As we have seen, this is the ethical experience of infinite responsibility at the heart of subjectivity, a moment of what I called *hetero-affectivity* prior to any auto-affection and disturbing any simple claim to autonomy. I also described this ethical experience in terms of conscience understood as a splitting at the heart of the self, a constitutive undoing and dispossessing of the self. As I tried to show in the last chapter, such an experience of conscience does not simply imply super-egoic cruelty, but is rather the experience of humorous self-division. This self-undoing is close to what Judith Butler has recently written about affect undoing us, in particular the affect of grief. In *Precarious Life*, Butler writes with great candour, 'Let's face it. We're undone by each other. And if we're not, we're missing something.'[47] Such an experience of grief is not depoliticizing, but on the contrary shows our essential interconnectedness and vulnerability to the other's demand. Butler goes on, 'In grief, we are held in *thrall* by the other'.[48] In grief and mourning we undergo an experience of affective self-dispossession or self-undoing that can provide the motivational force to enter into a political sequence. It is this meta-political moment that propels one into facing and facing down a wrong or confronting a situation of injustice, not through sovereign legal norms backed up with the threat of violence, but through an ethical responsiveness to the sheer precariousness of the other's face, of their injurability and our own. An ethical politics flows from our constitutive power-lessness in the face of the other.

To prevent any misunderstanding, by the word 'meta-political' I do not mean non-political or pre-political. Although ethics and politics can be analytically distinguished, we always face an ethical, political and indeed socio-cultural manifold, a synthesis if you will. There is no pure ethical experience and no simple deduction from ethics as the relation to the other to politics as a relation to all others, as Levinas sometimes appears to believe. If ethics without politics is empty, then politics without ethics is blind. The world that we have in sight overwhelms us with the difficult plurality of its demands. My view is that we need ethics in order to see what to do in a political situation.

It is in this connection that Levinas's thematic of anarchism takes on great interest, particularly the way this theme is handled by

Miguel Abensour when he speaks of an anarchic disturbance of politics.[49] Levinas introduces the notion of anarchy in 'Substitution', the pivotal chapter of *Otherwise than Being or Beyond Essence*, where it is employed as a name for that which precedes any principle or *archè*.[50] Levinas understands *archè* in philosophical terms where the first 'scientific' principle is the positing of the subject, as we saw in Chapter 1 in relation to Fichte. On this account, philosophy begins with the idea of intellectual intuition as the self-intuiting or self-positing of the subject in terms of activity. Gently chiding talk of 'subject-positions', we might say that the subject *is* position. The subject is self-positing, it puts itself in place through an act of will. This self-positing might be linked to the notion of the spontaneity of the subject in Kant's First Critique or the concept of autonomy in the Second Critique, what we saw Rawls describe above as Kant's 'aristocracy of all', where each moral subject would be sovereign over itself insofar as it was freely determined by the moral law. Further back in the history of philosophy, we might think of this self-positing in terms of the *res cogitans* in Descartes as the Archimedean point of certainty that arrests the movement of doubt in Descartes. On Levinas's view, it is the sovereign self-positing subject that has dominated modern philosophy. This is what I called above the 'autonomy orthodoxy', where the *archè* is understood as *autarchy*, as self-origination or self-legislation – we might want to add self-satisfaction to this list. For Levinas, the twentieth-century philosophical heir to this thought is Heidegger's fundamental ontology, where the anticipatory resoluteness of authentic Dasein is simply a more existential version of self-positing autarchy.[51]

For Levinas, on the contrary, ethical subjectivity is the experience of being affected by an other in a way that precedes consciousness and which places in question our spontaneity and sovereignty. Our autonomous majesty is deposed and decapitated, our autonomous self-binding is unbound and we are undone. Our posturing subject-position is deposed. It is in this sense that Levinas claims that the heteronomous ethical experience of the relation to the neighbour is anarchical, the other posits me under their demand despite myself and before any act of the will.

Amplifying this line of thought, the other concepts that Levinas links to anarchy are obsession and persecution, which might be linked to Butler's notion of grief as affective self-undoing. In obsession, consciousness is overwhelmed by an experience of alterity; it is 'a way of being affected which can in no way be invested by spontaneity'.[52] It is precisely this reversal of modern philosophy's understanding of the relation of consciousness to its objects that defines the experience of persecution, where the activity of the will is subverted by the passivity of an affective undergoing that marks the ethical subject. Levinas writes, 'anarchy is persecution'.[53] In a fascinating footnote to these pages of *Otherwise than Being*, Levinas comes close to defining what he means by anarchy in relation to its customary political signification:

> The notion of anarchy we are introducing here has a meaning prior to the political (or anti-political) meaning popularly ascribed to it. It cannot, under pain of contradiction, be set up as a principle (in the sense that anarchists understand it). Anarchy, unlike *archè*, cannot be sovereign. It can only disturb, albeit in a radical way, the State, prompting isolated moments of negation *without any* affirmation. The State, then, cannot set itself up as a Whole.[54]

Anarchy should not seek to mirror the archic sovereignty that it undermines. That is, it should not seek to set itself up as the new hegemonic principle of political organization, but remain the negation of totality and not the affirmation of a new totality. Anarchy is a radical disturbance of the state, a disruption of the state's attempt to set itself up or erect itself into a whole (*s'ériger en Tout*). In our terms, anarchy is the creation of interstitial distance within the state, the continual questioning from below of any attempt to establish order from above. We might say that ethical anarchy is the experience of the multiple singularities of the encounter with others that defines the experience of sociality. Each of these singularities overwhelms and undoes us and we can never do enough in response. Any attempt to order these singularities into a shoulder-to-shoulder 'fighting collectivity', as Carl Schmitt might say, is doomed to fail.[55] This is the anti-authoritarian kernal to Levinas's work.[56]

A new language of civil disobedience

With this Levinasian conception of anarchism as a disturbance of the state in mind, I would like to turn from anarchist ethics to political anarchism and in particular contemporary forms of anarchist political organization. It seems to me that the great virtue of contemporary anarchist practice is its spectacular, creative and imaginative disturbance of the state. Contemporary anarchists have created a new language of civil disobedience that combines street-theatre, festival, performance art and what might be described as forms of non-violent warfare. Recalling the argument of the previous chapter, what one sees in groups like Ya Basta! and Rebel Clown Army is carnivalesque humour deployed as a political strategy. David Graeber describes some of these phenomena with great wit:

> Ya Basta! for example is famous for its *tute bianche* or white-overalls tactics: men and women dressed in elaborate forms of padding, ranging from foam armour to inner tubes to rubber ducky floatation devices, helmets and chemical proof white jumpsuits (their British cousins are well-clad WOMBLES [white overalls building libertarian effective struggles, s.c.]). As this mock army pushes its way through police barricades, all the while protecting each other against injury or arrest, the ridi-

culous gear seems to reduce human beings to cartoon characters – misshapen, ungainly, foolish, large, indestructible. The effect is only increased when lines of costumed figures attack police with balloons and water pistols or, like the 'Pink Bloc' at Prague and elsewhere, dress as fairies and tickle them with feather dusters. At the American Party Conventions, Billionaires for Bush dressed in high-camp tuxedos and evening gowns and tried to press wads of fake money into the cops' pockets, thanking them for repressing dissent.[57]

These comical tactics hide a serious critical political intent: they exemplify the effective forging of horizontal chains of equivalence or collective will formation across diverse and otherwise conflicting protest groups. Deploying a politics of subversion, contemporary anarchist practice exercises a satirical pressure on the state in order to show that other forms of life are possible. Picking up on my thoughts about humour, it is the exposed, self-ridiculing and self-undermining character of these forms of protest that I find most compelling as opposed to the pious humorlessness of most forms of vanguardist active nihilism and some forms of contemporary protest (I name no names). Groups like the Pink Bloc or Billionaires for Bush are performing their *powerlessness* in the face of power in a profoundly powerful way.[58] Politically, humour is a powerless power that uses its position of weakness to expose those in power through forms of self-aware ridicule. This is why the strategy of non-violent warfare is so important. Of course, history is habitually written by the people with the guns and sticks and one cannot expect to defeat them with mocking satire and feather dusters. Yet, as the history of ultra-leftist active nihilism eloquently shows, one is lost the moment one picks up the guns and sticks. Anarchic political resistance should not seek to mimic and mirror the archic violent sovereignty it opposes. It is rather a question of the cultivation of a *pacifist* activism that deploys techniques of non-violent warfare or what we might even call 'tactical frivolity'. But – to adapt a phrase of Levinas – this is a difficult pacifism that constantly has to negotiate the limits of violence.

Graeber offers a useful distinction between Marxism and anarchism: Marxism is typically a theoretical or analytical discourse about revolutionary strategy, whereas anarchism can be understood as an ethical discourse about revolutionary practice.[59] It is this emphasis on ethics as a binding factor in political practice that interests me, as opposed to the silence or hostility to ethics that one finds in Marx's work and in many Marxist (Gramsci is an obvious exception) and post-Marxist thinkers. As Simon Tormey writes,

> What tends to characterize collectivist anarchist approaches to 'post-capitalism' is a perhaps healthy dose of optimism about human motivation and also an undogmatic or non-doctrinal approach to issues of social organization.[60]

Yet, surely anarchism is overwhelmingly concerned with freedom and autonomy and has little to do with a hyperbolic Levinasian anarchism of infinite responsibility? As I said in the introduction to this chapter, my hypothesis and hope is that what differentiates contemporary anarchist practice from its previous 1960s variant turns around the question of freedom versus responsibility. There is no doubt that 60s anarchism was libertarian and linked to the sexual revolution, liberation of the erotic instincts and what Herbert Marcuse called 'nonrepressive sublimation'.[61] Yet, contemporary anarchism can be seen as a powerful critique of the pseudo-libertarianism of contemporary neo-liberalism, where the sexual revolution has turned the culture industry into the sex industry – ask yourself, is there today anything less transgressive and more normalizing than pornography? One might say that contemporary anarchism is about responsibility, whether sexual, ecological or socio-economic; it flows from an experience of conscience about the manifold ways in which the West ravages the rest; it is an ethical outrage at the yawning inequality, impoverishment and disenfranchisment that is so palpable locally and globally. In my view, contemporary anarchism is an experience of democratization of the type described above, where what motivates political struggle is a shared experience of certain wrongs and a determination to right those wrongs. What ties together the highly disparate groups that make up demonstrations of the kind we have seen so often in recent years is not a common set of theoretical doctrines, such as Marxism, but rather a shared sense of grievance and wrong, namely that unrestrained multi-national corporate, military capitalism is wrong, that war is the wrong response to the grief of 9/11, etc., etc., etc. Strange as it may sound, perhaps contemporary anarchism is more Levinasian than Marcusean. It is an anarchism of the other human being who places me under a heteronomous demand rather than an anarchism of the autonomous self.

At the core of Graeber's whole case for anarchism is a recovery of the notion of direct democracy. The protesters in Seattle chanted 'this is what democracy looks like'.[62] Graeber goes on to claim that this anarchist recovery of direct democracy is nothing less than the aspiration 'to reinvent daily life as a whole'.[63] If this sounds not simply utopian but downright crazy, then maybe it is as American as apple pie (or the death penalty). One can find the idea of democracy as a way of life as far back as Thomas Paine's radical distinction of society from government in *Common Sense*, or again in John Dewey's 'Creative Democracy', written on his eightieth birthday at the dark moment of 1939:

> When I think of the conditions under which men and women are living in many foreign countries today, fear of espionage, with danger hanging over the meeting of friends for friendly conversation in private gatherings, I am inclined to believe that the heart and final guarantee of democracy is in free gatherings of neighbors on the street corner to discuss back and forth what is read in uncensored news of the day, and in gatherings of

friends in the living rooms of houses and apartments to converse freely with one another.[64]

Of course, with the introduction of emergency legislation significantly reducing civil liberties after 9/11, one might wonder whether those residents of what Richard Rorty describes as the rich North Atlantic democracies are living under conditions slightly closer to those in the 'foreign countries' that Dewey mentions. However, I think it is the very apple pie quality to Graeber's understanding of direct democracy that is problematic. The conceptual cornerstone for Graeber's notion of anarchist democratic self-organization is consensus, and behind that stand unquestioned and simply liberal conceptions of freedom and autonomy.[65] Indeed, the description of anarchist democratic procedures sounds as dull and emptily procedural as the parliamentarianism that it opposes, with its system of 'friendly amendments', 'blocking' and 'standing aside' procedures, not to mention 'breakouts', 'spokecouncils' and 'non-binding straw polls'.[66] Worthy as they are, all of these techniques aim towards the goal of consensus and are rooted in unquestioned conceptions of freedom and autonomy. Perhaps it is this cluster of concepts that we should rethink.[67]

Allow me a brief caveat on the use of the concept of autonomy, as it might be felt that it is disingenuous, or even inconsistent, to reject the autonomy orthodoxy, on the one hand, and embrace the idea of an anarchist politics on the other, as if the latter had nothing to do with autonomy. To avoid any misunderstanding, I am not seeking to rule out autonomy, particularly as a goal in political life. Rather, I am seeking to introduce a significant *qualification* into the concept of autonomy at the level of ethical experience. My position is that politics as an ethical practice should not assume a pre-given or taken-for-granted notion of autonomy, but is rather hetero-affectively interpellated by a demand that divides it and which impels it into political sequences whose goal would be the cultivation of autonomous spaces. As we will now see, a key concept in such a politics is not consensus but *dissensus*.[68]

Dissensus and anger

As discussed above with regard to Levinas, the problem with much traditional thinking about politics is that it is *archic*: it is obsessed with the moment of foundation, origination, declaration, or institution that is linked to the act of government, of sovereignty, of establishing a state. At the core of such an archic politics lies the act of *decision* that initiates a self-positing sovereign political subject capable of self-government and the government of others. Such is arguably the intent of a tradition of political philosophy that begins in Plato's *Republic* and which continues through Hobbes and up to Carl Schmitt. I would contend that political philosophy in this sense is essentially anti-political. In Hannah Arendt's terms it consists in the reduction of the political to the social, or in Jacques Rancière's terms it is the reduction of politics (*la politique*) to the order of the police (*la police*).[69] That is, the political manifestation of the people has to be policed. The people must be reduced to their allotted social or bureaucratically designated function in the state as soldier, worker or guardian – the social division of labour given in the *Republic* that reflects Plato's threefold division of the soul. This political Platonism finds a faithful and deeply troubling echo in Heidegger's 1933 *Rectoral Address*, with its numerous allusions to the *Republic* and its tripartite division of the student body into work service, military service, and knowledge service (*Arbeitsdienst, Wehrdienst, Wissensdienst*). Heidegger writes, and note where he places his emphases, 'The three bonds – *by* the people, to the destiny of the state, *in* a spiritual mission are *equally primordial* to the German essence.'[70]

What such a tradition of political thinking fears most is the people, the radical manifestation of the people. This does not mean the people as purported unity of *das Volk* or *le peuple* shaped by destiny of the state in accordance with their national essence. Rather, I mean the people as *die Leute*, or *les gens* in their irreducible plurality, what we saw Hegel call above the 'formless mass' of the people.

Who are the people? They are not, in my view, the expression of a national essence, the alleged unity of a race, the citizens of a nation-state, the members of a specific class like the proletariat, or indeed the members of a specific community defined by religion, ethnicity, or whatever. The people cannot be socially identified and policed by any territorializing term. Rather the people are what Rancière describes as that empty space, the supplement that exceeds any social quantification or accounting. The people are those who do not count, who have no right to govern whether through hereditary entitlement like the aristocracy or by wealth and property ownership like the bourgeoisie.[71] Politics is the manifestation of the multiplicity that is the people, of the uncounted *demos*. Although Rancière would doubtless disagree, I think this manifestation is anarchic in the sense in which Levinas speaks, already in *Totality and Infinity*, of 'the anarchy essential to multiplicity'.[72] To express this in unlovely jargon, such anarchy is the meta-political disturbance of the anti-political order of the police.

If the activity of government continually risks pacification, order, security and what Rancière refers to as the 'idyll of consensus', then politics consists in the manifestation of a dissensus that disturbs the order by which government wishes to depoliticize society.[73] My problem with Graeber's work is that I hear an echo of this depoliticization in his anarchism, a desire for consensus that ignores the constitutive dissensual antagonism of political life. Now, if politics can be understood as the manifestation of the anarchic demos, then politics and democracy are two names for the same thing. Thus, democracy is not a fixed political form of society, but rather what I called above the *deformation* of society from itself through the act of material political manifestation. Democracy is a political process, the movement of democratization, which comes close to the idea of direct democracy but without the apple pie. On my view, democratization consists in the manifestation of dissensus, in demonstration as *demos*-stration, manifesting the presence of those who do not count. Democratization is politicization, it is the cultivation of what might be called *politicities*, zones of hegemonic struggle that work against the consensual idyll of the state. Such a disturbance of the state does not have to be teleologically linked to the construction of an archic nation-subject, but rather towards the cultivation of an anarchic multiplicity.[74]

deconstruction

Ethics is anarchic meta-politics. It is the anarchic moment of democratic dissensus articulated around the experience of the ethical demand, the exorbitant demand at the heart of my subjectivity that defines that subjectivity by dividing it and opening it to otherness. This demand is not some theoretical abstraction. My discussion of Marx has hopefully made clear the way in which this demand takes place in a situation, a situation of globalized exploitation, a situation of what I called in the first words of this book, 'political disappointment'. This disappointment provokes an experience of injustice and the feeling of *anger*. I think anger is very important, and, contrary to the classical tradition, in Seneca say, I think it is the first political emotion. It is often anger that moves the subject to action. Anger is the emotion that produces motion, the mood that moves the subject. But such anger at the multiple injustices and wrongs of the present provokes an ethical response. The problem with contemporary ethics, particularly the horribly devalued currencies of freedom, human rights and liberal democracy is, as Chantal Mouffe rightly says, the risk of a moralization of politics and hence the risk of depoliticization.[75] I completely agree, but I do not think that the fact of moralization should lead to the suspension of ethics. On the contrary, I think it should lead to the development of alternative ethical frameworks. It might indeed lead to the cultivation of an infinitely demanding ethics of commitment and political resistance that can face and face down depoliticizing moralization. Such is the wager of this book.

Conclusion

How might a politics of the type I have described happen? How might it become effective? One might say that politics just happens, but that it is not happening now, ours are not favourable times. One might say, like some post-Heideggerian leftists, that it is necessary to cultivate the ethos of thinking without the destructive will to mastery, to wait and await the advent of the saving power of the revolution that may one day come to pass. One might say, like some post-Benjaminian leftists, that Auschwitz or the death camps are the *nomos* of a modernity that is characterized by the worldwide deployment of a state of exception and the mythic violence of law where all we can do is attend to the faintest potentiality of the unpredictable divine violence of revolution. One might say, like some post-Althusserian leftists, that politics is rare or even eclipsed, the last great example being 1968, and we have to acknowledge that we are living in a de-politicized, post-democratic era of generalized nihilism. One might say, like some post-Lacanian leftists, that we must maintain the dialectical double-vision of the parallax view while implicitly acknowledging that this position is little more than the expression of a massive philosophical and political *deadlock*. But one might also simply, sharply and strongly disagree with these positions and say the following: politics is not rare or seldom and to adopt such a position is finally defeatist. Politics is now and many. The massive structural dislocations of our times can invite pessimism, even forms of active or passive nihilism as I emphasized at the beginning of this book, but they can also invite militancy and optimism, an invitation for our capacity of political invention and imagination, an invitation, finally, for our ethical commitment and political resistance.

In order not to be defeatist, in order not to participate in what we might call the 'Eeyorism' that is the self-negating speciality of the intellectual left, in order to be affirmative and even a little optimistic, I think we have to acknowledge that such a conception of politics requires an account of motivational force that is irreducibly ethical. On my view, ethics is the experience of an infinite demand at the heart of my subjectivity, a demand that undoes me and requires me to do more, not in the name of some sovereign authority, but in the namelessness of a powerless exposure, a vulnerability, a responsive responsibility, a humorous self-division. Politics is not the naked operation of power or an ethics-free agonism, it is an ethical practice that is driven by a response to situated injustices and wrongs.

In these dark times of war, in this period of the increasingly desperate shoring up of the *imperium*, we can no longer trust our political destiny to the quasi-automatic inner contradictions of socio-economic laws of motion, to a spontaneously emerging social actor who would overthrow the state. Marxist economism has to be contested as vigorously as its neo-liberal big brother. Nor can our guide in politics be some set of ontological or metaphysical presuppositions, whether Heidegger's notion of the completion of metaphysics in technology, Marx's notion of species-being, the purportedly emancipatory effulgence of the multitude, or whatever. No revolution is going to be generated out of systemic or structural laws. We are on our own and what we do we have to do for ourselves. Politics requires subjective invention, imagination and endurance, not to mention tenacity and cunning. No ontology or eschatological philosophy of history is going to do it for us. Working at an interstitial distance from the state, a distance that I have tried to describe as democratic, we need to construct political subjectivities that are not arbitrary or relativistic, but which are articulations of an ethical demand whose scope is universal and whose evidence is faced in a concrete situation. This is dirty, detailed, local, practical and largely unthrilling work. It is time we made a start.

Appendix: Crypto-Schmittianism – the Logic of the Political in Bush's America[1]

My question is very simple, but the answer is far from self-evident: how do we begin to grasp the political situation in which we find ourselves? It is politics that I would like to talk about, or more precisely the logic of the political. More precisely still, my concern is the logic of the political as it is deployed by the Bush administration in the USA. The concept that I want to advance in order to get a grip on that logic, a concept that I hope has some explanatory power, is what I call 'crypto-Schmittianism', which I will explain presently.

Let's begin by asking the obvious question: how did Bush get reelected in the American Presidential elections in November 2004? How did Bush win? Well, I think part of the story is that certain people in the Bush administration have got a clear, robust and powerful understanding of the nature of the political. They have read their Machiavelli, their Hobbes, their Leo Strauss and misread their Nietzsche. They understand the more or less noble lies that need to be told in order to secure and keep hold of political power. In their hands, some of the most precious words we have – democracy, rights, human dignity and most of all freedom – have been twisted and debased into ignoble lies that are told in order to maintain political power. But, worse still, certain people in the Bush administration have read their Carl Schmitt.[2] They understand that politics (and this might serve as a definition) is a sphere of activity that acts through force, generally founded on law – but not always, not in a time of emergency or a state of exception when the sovereign is he who makes the law as was the case in Guantanamo. The political is a sphere of activity which is concerned with the external security and the internal order of a political unit, what we usually call a state, whether local, national or imperial. Furthermore, the political is that activity that assures the internal order of a political unit like the imperial state through the more or less fantastic threat of an enemy. The political is about the construction of an enemy in order to maintain the unity of the citizenry. That is to say, the unity of the citizens, in this case Americans, is constituted through the relation to an enemy. Post-9/11, that is, post-Cold War and the disappearance of the communist enemy, this role has obviously been taken over by what is called international terrorism: Osama bin Laden, Saddam Hussein, or whatever fantasy fusion of these beings was melded in the minds of the electorate, or more recently by figures like Abu Musab al-Zarqawi, killed in June 2006. There is a double fantasy going on here: the fantasy of the enemy and the fantasy of the homeland. Furthermore, it is through the fantasy of the enemy that the fantasy of the homeland is constituted.

Politics has arguably always been conducted at the level of fantasy, the image and spectacle, but it is particularly egregious at the present time. Indeed, what unites the Bush Administration and al-Qaeda is their obsession with the spectacle, a painful love affair with the image, both the image of empire's spectacular defeat with the destruction of the World Trade Center and the attack on the Pentagon, and the attempt to respond to that defeat with the image of 'shock and awe' in the conflicts in Afghanistan and Iraq (I will come back to the theme of awe); both the carefully controlled and choreographed video appearances of Osama bin Laden sitting cross-legged in a cave and speaking softly with an AK 47 propped up behind him, or 'W' strutting and smiling in combat fatigues on an aircraft carrier to declare a highly premature end to hostilities.

Politics is more than ever concerned with the spectacle and the control of the image, which is what makes the Situationism of Guy Debord more relevant than ever as a diagnostic tool in political analysis. Yet, there is a contradiction to the present, namely that it is characterized by an utter pervasiveness of the spectacle, yet what that spectacle reveals is a social process that is hollow to the core, where the reality it offers its subjects is that of Reality TV. Paradoxically, this obsession with the image is never truer than in conditions of seeming invisibility. I was in London for the bombings of 7th July 2005, which were on the subway system and therefore invisible as I walked into Central London on that bright and lovely summer morning. But 7/7, as it is unfortunately being called, is all about the control of visibility, whether the images taken on cell phones from people trapped on trains, which were graphic and terrifying in their grainy, poor quality, or the images of terrorist suspects, one wearing a New York hooded top, that were captured by the surveillance cameras that survey almost every inch of London (it is estimated that one is photographed by surveillance cameras between twenty and thirty times if one travels from one side of London to the other). Other recent examples of politics as the control of visibility are obviously the aftermath of Hurricane Katrina in late August and September 2005 and the seeming 'shock appearance' of Black urban poverty and distress, and the entire Danish cartoon affair that rumbled on throughout the Winter 2005–6, where the battleground of visibility took place at the level of caricature.

Let's be clear what I am saying: first, order and security have become systematically blurred, where order is security: security of the fantasy of the homeland from the fantasy of the enemy through the control of the means for the production of the spectacle. Second, to grasp the logic of the political is to understand that order and security are maintained through the opposition to an enemy, an enemy at once real and fantastical, a sort of shadowy imago that can strike at the heart of the place you call home at any and every moment. Which is to say that politics is essentially about the management of fear, an economy of fear, continually adjusting the level of fear to produce the right level of affect in the citizenry. I'm thinking of economy in Freud's sense here, as the regulation of the right distribution of energy, of affective flow, in the psycho-political organism. It seems to me that there is a desperate need at the present time for the development of a discipline that we might call 'political psychology' or 'political psychoanalysis'.

Once again, this idea of politics as the management of fear is nothing new; just think of Spinoza's cautionary words about fear, superstition and the boundless credulity of human beings in times of crisis at the beginning of the *Theological-Political Treatise*.[3] Of course, the University of Chicago educated reactionaries in the Bush Administration have also read their classical literature. It is the lesson of Aeschylus' *Oresteia*. As you will recall, the *Oresteia* is a thoroughly political tragedy concerned with the nature of justice in the state, with what is right for the Athenians at the moment of their imperial ambition, their imperial extension and projection of power. At the end of the drama, Athena, the arbiter of justice, a sort of one-woman-goddess version of the Supreme Court, says

> Neither anarchy nor tyranny, my people.
> Worship the mean, I urge you,
> Shore it up with reverence and never
> Banish terror from the gates, not outright.
> Where is the righteous man who knows no fear?
> The stronger your fear, your reverence for the just,
> The stronger your country's wall and city's safety.[4]

Shore up the mean with reverence *and* terror, but never banish terror from the gates of the state. The stronger the fear, the stronger the reverence for the just, the stronger your country's wall and the city's safety. A safer world, a more hopeful America, to recall the slogan of the brilliantly, indeed spectacularly, well-

managed Republican National Convention in New York in September 2004. The political as the strength of the country's wall is
maintained through an economy of fear and an economy of terror.
The lesson of Aeschylus was not lost on Hobbes. He writes:

> For if we could suppose a great Multitude of men to consent in
> the observation of Justice, and other Lawes of Nature, without a
> common Power to keep them in awe; we might as well suppose
> all Man-kind to do the same; and then there neither would be,
> nor need to be, any Civill Government, or Common-wealth at
> all; because there would be Peace without subjection.[5]

Of course, for Hobbes, the idea of peace without subjection is
ludicrous and we require the common power of the commonwealth in order to escape the state of war. Such is the function of
the sovereign, where sovereign power completes the circuit of
subjection through the feeling of awe, through what Donald
Rumsfeld called in 2003 'shock and awe'. The social glue that
binds subjects peacefully is a reverential fear for the sovereign.
Listen to the way in which Hobbes describes him: 'He hath the use
of so much Power and Strength conferred on him, that by terror
thereof, he is inabled to form the wills of all . . . And in him
consisteth the Essence of the Commonwealth'.[6] By terror
thereof . . . the sovereign has the ability, the potency and the
virility to form the will of all. This is the essence of the commonwealth, of the so-called social contract, what Rousseau calls in the
Second Discourse 'the fraudulent social contract'.[7] Peace is nothing more but the regulation of the psycho-political economy of awe
and reverential fear, of using the threat of terror in order to bind
citizens to the circuit of their subjection.

Who can forget the wonderful Leslie Nielsen character in *Police
Squad*, whose slogan was 'I'm interested in justice, and that means
bullets'? The political leader – the modern day Prince – understands this and knows how to operate an economy of terror and

how to use violence. He knows justice means bullets, and he knows how to conduct an overseas war with a fantastical enemy. If 100,000 or so Iraqis die in the process and a few thousand of the disenfranchised *Lumpenproletariat*, then that is a small price to pay for four more years of power. And to think that many, many people, intelligent and well-meaning people, people on the 2003 anti-war marches, people all over the world, even some of the titanic intellects on the faculty at the New School where I work, had the stupidity to describe George Bush as stupid. He is not stupid. Calling him stupid is stupid. What took place in the lead up to the last Presidential elections in 2004 was the exercise of genuine political intelligence which comes out of a rich understanding of a classical tradition of thinking the political.

*

Yet, what I have just said doesn't really get at the phenomenon in the right way. I would argue that what characterizes the concept of the political in the Bush administration is not so much Schmittian-ism as what I want to call 'crypto-Schmittianism'. What do I mean by that? Roughly the following: on the one hand, the concept of the political is based on the fantasy construction of the enemy, main-taining the economy of awe and terror that allows order to be secured in the so-called homeland. On the other hand, the decisive feature that defines the current US administration is a thorough-going hypocrisy about the political. What I mean is that, in Carl Schmitt's terms, there is something chronically *depoliticizing* about the ideology of the current administration. Going back to those ignoble lies that are being told, contemporary US imperial power espouses an utterly moralizing, universalist, indeed millennial, ideology whose key signifier is freedom. I will come back to freedom. Allied to freedom are notions of democracy and human rights and they even have the audacity to speak about human dignity in the 2002 National Security Strategy document that provided the metaphysical justification for pre-emptive military action in Afghanistan and Iraq.[8] Not far behind these signifiers lies the crucial question of faith and the link between faith and politics, or the triangulation of a faith that permits a moralization of political judgements on a metaphysical basis. The astonishing and much-discussed factoid about the presence of moral values in the exit polls from November 2004 and which caused a minor panic amongst American liberals, is deeply interesting to a humble philosopher. Citizens are making political decisions that are really moral judgements and these judgements flow from a dogmatic metaphysics, to be precise God as the depoliticizing instance par excellence. Once again, to bang this point home, this is not stupid. To critical, secular, well-dressed metro-sexual post-Kantians like us, this view of the world might well appear deluded, indeed we might think that a pro-life, anti-queer metaphysics is downright pernicious, but there is no doubt that the triangulation of faith, morality and politics is a framework of intelligibility that makes powerful sense. To go further, one might say that the strong connection between faith, morality and politics is one of the most enduring features of civil society in the US since the time of the original violent settlement, through to the eulogies of Tom Paine and Tocqueville. The left ignores that connection at its peril.

Of course, what we are broaching here is the question of civil religion, and in particular civil religion in Rousseau's political theory, the extraordinary final chapter of *The Social Contract*, which got him into such trouble with the authorities in Paris and Geneva after its publication in 1762.[9] Rousseau thought, and rightly, that religion was the unifying ideological glue in any legitimate polity. What got him into trouble was his conviction – and this was a century before Nietzsche – that Christianity was unfit for this purpose as it directed citizens' attention away from this world to the afterworld and the care of their immortal soul. What Rousseau tackles with alarming directness is the problem of Christianity and politics, namely the Christian separation of theological and political authority. In the religions of antiquity there was an identity of theological and political authority. One need only read the *Oresteia* or the tragedies of Sophocles to realize that the gods of the Athenians were gods of the city, civic gods without any universal jurisdiction. Although cities and peoples were jealously proud of their local gods, this pride went hand in hand with the recognition of the relativity of religious belief; namely, that the gods of Sparta were not the gods of Athens or Corinth and furthermore the adoption of such gods would not be good for the Athenians, the Corinthians or anyone else. Oddly, this relativity of belief never seems to have led to religious war. Christianity, by contrast, which requires universality of belief has led to little else but religious wars for the past couple of millennia. Christianity divides political and theological authority, declaring that the kingdom of God is not of this world, but of the next. It is an essentially anti-political religion. Rousseau declares, 'After all, what does it matter whether one is free or a slave in this vale of tears?' He goes on, 'Far from attaching the hearts of the citizens to the state, this religion [i.e. Christianity] detaches them from it as from all other things of this world; and I know of nothing more contrary to the social spirit.'[10] In an eerie anticipation of Nietzsche's argument in *On the Genealogy of Morals*, Rousseau writes that Christianity is slave morality, 'True Christians are made to be slaves; they know it and they hardly care; this short life has too little value in their eyes.'[11]

In the US, what passes for Christianity – and it is, to say the least, a highly perverse, possessive individualist and capitalist version of what I would see as Christ's messianic ethical communism – is a new civil religion, a civil religion of freedom. An essential reference point for American civil religion is Robert Bellah's classic 1975 book, written during the Vietnam war, *The Broken Covenant: American Civil Religion in Time of Trial.*[12] Bellah argues that what is distinctive about American Christianity is its fusion of two traditions: Massachusetts Puritanism and Virginian Roman republicanism, which is architecturally expressed in the public buildings of

Washington DC. In this regard, consider George W. Bush's inaugural speech as President on January 20th 2005, with its multiple – in fact more than forty – references to either freedom or liberty in seventeen minutes of slow and passionless oratory.[13] There is some evidence that Bush worked hard on this speech and he even seems to have read a book. Unfortunately, that book was by Natan Sharansky, former Minister in Ariel Sharon's administration, *The Case for Democracy: The Power of Freedom to Overcome Tyranny and Terror*.[14] Bush presents three theses:

(i) For Bush, the only emancipatory force in human history is human freedom and 'self-government relies, in the end, on the governing of the self', i.e. self-legislation or autonomy.

(ii) Yet, the so-called 'author of liberty' is God who stands outside human affairs. For Bush, God plays the role that Rousseau assigns to the lawgiver, the stranger or foreigner figure that legislates for the community. What we might call, with Agamben, the paradox of sovereignty is that human freedom is only guaranteed by a theological agency that both ordains and constrains that freedom.

(iii) Furthermore, Bush goes on in a much more Hegelian or Fukuyaman direction than Rousseau, arguing that the 'author of liberty' gives history direction and purpose. History, it would appear, is the eschatology of freedom. Let's just say that I have grave doubts about this position, but there is no denying the coherence and political classicism of this worldview.

There are huge theological problems in the invocation of Christianity in contemporary US politics. The idea that the mission (I use the word advisedly) of politics is the expansion of freedom and that freedom is a gift from God is a doctrine that sits very oddly with the history and dogma of the Christian church. For the latter, freedom is more of a problem that a solution, being nothing more than the capacity to err that is the consequence of our post-lapsarian state. Christian freedom has to be disciplined by a life of withdrawal, prayer and asceticism that can do no more than hope for the very opposite of freedom, namely the dispensation of divine grace. It is clear that what Bush and his camp followers have very effectively done is to transform Christianity into an imperial civil religion with considerable populist appeal, particularly around core moral issues of opposition to abortion and gay marriage.

Let me try and summarize crypto-Schmittianism with an anecdote. In his book, *Plan of Attack*, the distinguished veteran journalist Bob Woodward asked 'W' if he talked to his father before going to war in Iraq.[15] He replied in the negative, but added that he had consulted a higher father. This is both funny and psychoanalytically revealing, I think. Above his 'real' father – Bush 1 – and even above his symbolic father – Reagan, whose death was spectacularly mourned in the US, as if he were truly the Christ of Bush II's civil religion, where Bush II assumes the role of St Peter – lies the divine father who ordains freedom in a castrating legislative act like the Big Other in Lacanian theory. However, Bush's response to Woodward's question is deeply serious and I have no reason to doubt 'W's' moral and theological sincerity. It reveals that a political decision of the classic friend–enemy variety is being made on the basis of the depoliticizing instance of God's will. The considerable power of this kind of political thinking (and – lest we forget – it is the justifying logic of most colonialism, which is what leads one to conclude that so much contemporary politics is simply neo-colonial) is that the enemy is not just, as in classical war, unlike us, or advancing a territorial claim that we want to repel, or blocking a territorial claim that we want to make. On the contrary, on the crypto-Schmittian view, the enemy is evil and becomes, in Schmitt's words, an outlaw of humanity, an outlaw who can therefore be legitimately annihilated in the name of freedom.[16] Might it not be the defining characteristic of contemporary essentially economic wars, that they are fought around the signifier of humanity? And might not the presence of this signifier be the key to understanding the savage inhumanity of contemporary war? And although I do not think that philosophers should be in the business of prediction and prophecy, there is little doubt in my mind that future wars (and there *will* be future wars without significant geo-political transformation) will also be economic wars fought for the possession of scarce commodities, notably oil as the key global commodity. Recall Schmitt's phrase, adapted from Proudhon, 'Whoever invokes humanity wants to cheat.'[17] I think this means that the slightly further left amongst us should also be careful about invoking the signifier of humanity in any oppositional politics. As the great Portuguese poet, Fernando Pessoa, writes:

> They spoke to me of people, and of humanity.
> But I've never seen people, or humanity.
> I've seen various people, astonishingly dissimilar,
> Each separated from the next by unpeopled space.[18]

*

To summarize my main point, the Bush administration has a clear and strong understanding of the political, but this is wrapped up in a moralizing, depoliticized discourse. This combination is hypo-critical but politically extremely very effective. It is, indeed, lethal to its enemies. How then does one oppose it? What, at this point in time, are the possibilities of oppositional politics?

Let me begin by turning to the Democratic Party. The problem with them is that they are too decent, too gentlemanly or gentle-womanly. They are too nice. They want to bring healing and reconciliation to the divided body politic. They want to take the country back, as they somewhat whimsically tend to say. It seems to me that they don't understand a damn thing about the political. They need to understand the savagery of politics. They need political teeth, not soft lips and smiles. They capitulate too easily and if they continue in that manner they will simply limp from well-meaning defeat to well-meaning defeat. They need to study their Carl Schmitt and, more importantly, Gramsci on common sense, hegemony, religion, ideology and collective will formation, and they need to quietly slip their John Rawls back on the bookshelf. It sometimes seems to me that the only thing in which many American leftists believe, particularly the Habermasians squirming in their seats since 9/11, is law, particularly international law. International law is a very nice thing, but if it fails to have an anchor in everyday social practices then it leads to a politics of abstraction. Incidentally, this is also how I would view the rejection of the European Constitution in the referenda in France and the Netherlands, where the various governmental and bureaucratic elites thought they could simply override the popular will. Of course, in the referenda the opposite happened and the consequences for the European Union are serious and far-reaching as many European countries reject what they see as multiculturalism and slip back into some atavistic nationalist discourse. The lesson of the above for the left, wherever it may be, is that the *sine qua non* of oppositional politics lies in an understanding of populism, what Gramsci used to call the 'national-popular'. What needs to be politically articulated at this historical conjuncture is, in my view, a leftist populism.[19]

On the question of an oppositional, leftist political strategy in the US context, everything depends on having a clear view of what or who we are dealing with here, namely the nature of the right, the religious right or the radical right. At least provisionally, it seems to me that there are two options:

1. The religious right is undoubtedly a huge bolus in contemporary American politics, but it is moveable, it is digestable, it can be excreted. Although, it is a force in politics that has been gaining an ever more powerful momentum since the Reagan years, it is not necessarily a permanent feature of the political landscape.

2. The religious right is what my colleague Anne Stoler has called a new regime of truth, a new framework of intelligibility that is not stupid. It is rather a new theologico-political form of life, a new conception of the world that will, in the future, assert more and more influence in American political life.

What follows from this? If option 1 is true, then I think it is arguable that we should stay within the traditional party political structure, hopefully in a more radicalized manner, and try and make the Democratic Party electable by bringing 'Jesusland' with us. I really hope that option 1 is right, because if option 2 is right, then we are witnessing the birth of some rough new beast slouching its way towards us. To deal with this beast, we need to sharpen our best sociological, anthropological, historical and analytical tools, but we have the face the awkward truth that if we are entering a new regime of truth, then this poses a potentially devastating threat to what we comfortingly think of as the liberal polity.

In addition to the logic of the external enemy, we might put this together with the issue of the internal enemy, which I haven't discussed, what the Right would call 'the culture of death' that is opposed to Bush and the dead Pope's so-called 'culture of life'. This culture of death would include those purportedly amoral, value-free nihilistic east and west coasts, dens of iniquity like Greenwich Village and Berkeley, full of queers, Jews and resident aliens, relentlessly aborting fetuses while being metaphysically uncertain, perhaps even atheistic. If we place the internal and external enemy side-by-side, then the picture starts to look very nasty indeed. The United States is effectively disunited and divided into what William Connolly and I have baptized 'Puritania' on the one hand and 'Pluristan' on the other.

Let me finish by trying to identify the live political options at the present time. In order to do this, I would like to borrow from an important intervention entitled *Afflicted Powers: Capital and Spectacle in a New Age of War*, written by the Retort group based in San Francisco.[20]

As I see it, there are at least three live political options at the present time, although this list does not pretend to be exhaustive:

1. What we might call *military neo-liberalism*, whether the nasty sort we have seen with Bush Jr. or the slightly softer, but not enormously different, Democratic Party version of this, provided they succeed in finding a new Clinton, and he was no stranger to bombing, lest it be forgotten. Military neo-liberalism is also a fitting description of Blair's New Labour project, all mainstream British politics, and a good deal of European politics, with some noble exceptions. Let me state categorically and melancholically that I have every reason to believe that military neo-liberalism will dominate the future. I very much hope not, but it is the sad lesson of history that it is usually written by the people with the guns and sticks.

2. What I would like to call *neo-Leninism*, which is practically expressed in the vanguardism of groups like al-Qaeda. As I claimed in the Introduction to this book, the left should approach al-Qaeda with the words and actions of bin Laden resonating against those of Lenin, Blanqui, Mao, Baader-Meinhoff and Durrutti. I see Jihadist revolutionary Islam as a novel and highly effective continuation of classical forms of revolutionary vanguardism. I am deeply suspicious of such forms of revolutionary vanguardism, in particular as concerns their use of violence. As a character in Jean-Luc Godard's *Notre musique* puts it, 'Tuer un homme pour défendre une idée, n'est pas de défendre une idée, c'est tuer un homme' ('To kill a human being in order to defend an idea is not to defend an idea, it is to kill a human being').[21] Or, as Subcommandante Marcos of the Zapatistas succinctly expressed it in a 2003 communiqué to ETA, the Basque separatist organization, 'I shit on all the revolutionary vanguards of this planet.'[22]

3. The political phenomenon that frames *Afflicted Powers* is the 2003 anti-war demonstrations and there is no question that these and other phenomena indicate that something has decisively shifted in the nature and tactics of resistance. The authors of *Afflicted Powers* somewhat half-heartedly describe this non-vanguardist left in terms of Hardt and Negri's notion of the multitude, and I think this is perhaps the weakest point of their argument. Without wishing to rehearse arguments laid out in the final chapter of this book, I would dispute the claim that the multitude is the new political subject and political alternative that grows within empire on both theoretical and political grounds.

Theoretically, the analysis given in Hardt and Negri's *Empire* at the ontological level risks retreating into the very anti-dialectical materialist ontology of substance that Marx rightly criticized in his early work. Politically, Hardt and Negri's approach makes the work of politics too systemic where both empire and multitude, that is, both capitalism and the resistance to capitalism, originate in the same ontological substance. As I argued above, politics is a disruption of the ontological domain and separate categories are required for its analysis and practice.

Returning to the third option, I would want to describe it as what we might call *neo-anarchism*. Such a neo-anarchism is concerned with the mobilization of a multiplicity, but I would hesitate to call it a multitude because that would risk ontologizing politics, seeing politics as the expression of some common substance, which is as depoliticizing a gesture as I can imagine. What interests me in contemporary anarchism is the cultivation of a highly spectacular tactics of protest, the forging of a new language of civil disobedience or what I called above, following David Graeber, 'non-violent warfare', where I want to emphasize the words 'non-violent'. If what unites military neo-liberalism and neo-Leninism is a commitment to violence, then an opposition to both has to be committed to non-violence, to a practice and activity of peace. Regardless of any ontologistic theodicy, politics is the activity of the

forming of a common front, the horizontal aggregation of a
collective will from diverse groups with disparate demands. Such
a neo-anarchism, which is what makes it neo-, cannot hope to
achieve the classical anarchist dream of society without the state,
which I simply do not think is an option for most of the earth's
population at this point in time. But such a neo-anarchist experience of the political can articulate a politics at a distance from the
state, what I call above an *interstitial distance* within and against the
state. Resistance is about the articulation of distance, the creation
of space or spaces of distance from the state, what the very young
Marx calls 'true democracy' in his critique of Hegel's philosophy of
the state. Indeed, it is in these terms that I would want to describe
some of the new social mobilizations, such as the movements for an
alternative globalization and indigenous rights discussed in the final
chapter of this book. On my view, at the core of such a neo-
anarchism, there is not an ontology, nor an economistic theodicy,
but an infinitely demanding ethics of commitment that challenges
the vapid mantras of contemporary ideological moralism.

Explanatory note

Like elephant pregnancies, most books have long gestation periods. This one is no exception. It is the distillation into a single, continuous argument of much that I have been thinking and writing about for many years, at least since my time as a PhD student in the late 1980s. My aim is very simple: to lay out my position on ethics as clearly and persuasively as possible and to show how that position has, I hope, significant political consequences. In the Introduction and Appendix, I frame the book with a philosophical and political *Zeitdiagnose* where I humbly try to comprehend our time in thought and analyse the socio-political context that motivates my argument

Although I have been fortunate enough to present either parts or the whole of this book in numerous contexts in recent years, the occasion to bring my thoughts on ethics and politics together into a short book was provided by several happy consequences of my move to New York in 2004. First, the manuscript was developed in weekly lectures on ethics in 2004 and during two seminar courses on politics in 2004 and 2006 at the New School for Social Research, the second co-taught with Rainer Forst. I am deeply grateful to New School graduate students for creating a space of intellectual intensity the like of which I had never previously experienced. Second, the invitation to give the 2004 Albert Schweizer Lectures on Ethics and Politics at New York University provided a catalyst for many of my arguments and allowed me to shape my thoughts. I am grateful to Gabriela Basterra for organizing these lectures and for responding to my work. In addition, I would like to acknowledge the work of the Radical Politics group at the University of Essex in 2003 and the Anarchist Reading Group in New York in 2006. Vital interlocutors along the way have been Emily Apter, Alain Badiou, Jay Bernstein, Jacob Blumenfeld, Anne Deneys-Tunney, Lisabeth During, Bernard Flynn, Kristin Gissberg, Peter Goodrich, David Graeber, Courtney Jung, Elliot Jurist, Andreas Kalyvas, Ernesto Laclau, Abraham Mansbach, Michael Morgan, Daniel Morris, Thamy Pogrebinschi, Ross Poole, Mark Thorsby, Mitchell Verter, Judith Walz and – last but first – Jamieson Webster.

Careful readers will find the recapitulation of arguments from elsewhere in my work that I here hope to bring together in a more systematic, direct and forceful presentation. I have borrowed from the Preface to the Second Edition of *Very Little . . . Almost Nothing* (London and New York: Routledge 2004); from Chapters 8, 9 and 10 of *Ethics–Politics–Subjectivity* (London and New York: Verso, 1999), which is being reprinted to accompany the publication of this book; and, in particular, from Chapter 7 of *On Humour* (London and New York: Routledge, 2002). I have also adapted and rewritten sections from the following papers: 'Five problems in Levinas's view of politics and the sketch of a solution to them', *Political Theory*, Volume 32, No.2 (April 2004); 'Demanding Approval: On the Ethics of Alain Badiou', *Radical Philosophy* No.100 (March 2000); and 'Is there a Normative Deficit in the Theory of Hegemony?', in *Ernesto Laclau – A Critical Reader*, eds. S. Critchley and O. Marchart (London & New York: Routledge, 2004). At Verso, I would like to thank Tom Penn and Robin Blackburn for their help, interest and guidance.

Simon Critchley
New York City, August 2006.

Notes

Introduction

1 As might be clear, the role of the passive nihilist is being played by John Gray. See his *Straw Dogs* (London: Granta, 2002) and *The Necessity of Myth* (Maastricht: Studium Generale, 2003).

2 I here follow the analysis of revolutionary Islam given by the Retort group in *Afflicted Powers: Capital and Spectacle in a New Age of War* (London and New York: Verso, 2005), see esp. Ch.5, pp.132–69.

3 In this connection, see Bruce Lawrence's enormously illuminating edition of bin Laden's writings, *Messages to the World. The Statements of Osama bin Laden* (London and New York: Verso, 2005), esp. pp.xx–xxiii.

4 Of course, and crucially, it should also be recognized that this motivational deficit with respect to the institutions of liberal democracy, in particular with regard to electoral politics, has also had positive effects, which I will analyse in the final chapter with respect to indigenous rights movements and movements critical of neo-liberal globalization. It has led increasing numbers of citizens to become dissatisfied with established authorities and traditional hierarchical institutions and to engage in non-electoral political activities, such as the dramatic explosion in numbers of NGOs and the developments of various networked groups of activists. Thus, the demotivating effects of liberal democracy can also be politically *remotivating*. The purpose of this book is to provide a conception of ethics that might support this remotivation.

5 See Jay Bernstein's *Adorno: Disenchantment and Ethics* (Cambridge: Cambridge University Press, 2001). In this connection, see also Ross Poole, *Morality and Modernity* (London and New York: Routledge, 1991).

6 See the interview with Foucault in 1984, the year of his death, 'The Ethics of the Concern of the Self as a Practice of Freedom', in Michel Foucault, *Ethics: Subjectivity and Truth*, ed. P. Rabinow (New York: The New Press, 1997), pp.281–301.

1   Demanding approval

1 See 'The Concept of Moral Insight and Kant's Doctrine of the Fact of
   Reason', in Dieter Henrich, *The Unity of Reason*, ed. Richard Velkley
   (Cambridge, Mass.: Harvard University Press, 1994), pp.55–87.
2 Romans 7:19.
3 Nietzsche, *On the Genealogy of Morals*, trans. R.J. Hollingdale & W.
   Kaufmann (New York: Vintage, 1969) p.82.
4 See Honneth's Preface to *The Fragmented World of the Social* (Albany:
   SUNY Press, 1995).
5 Francis Hutcheson, *On the Nature and Conduct of the Passions with Illustrations
   of the Moral Sense*, ed. A. Ward (Manchester: Clinamen Press, 1999
   [1728]).
6 On this point, see Alasdair MacIntyre, *A Short History of Ethics* (London:
   Macmillan, 1966), p.162–3.
7 Michael Smith, *The Moral Problem* (Oxford: Blackwell, 1994).
8 Cited in Henrich, op.cit., p.73.
9 Kant introduces and defines the fact of reason in the *Critique of Practical
   Reason*, trans. Lewis White Beck (Indianapolis: Bobbs-Merrill, 1956),
   p.31. For a powerfully robust recent discussion of the fact of reason, from
   which I nonetheless dissent, see Rainer Forst, 'Moralische Autonomie
   und Autonomie der Moral. Zu einer Theorie der Normativität nach
   Kant', *Deutsche Zeitschrift für Philosophie*, 52 (2004), no.2, pp.179–97.
10 Kant, *Critique of Practical Reason*, p.47. Emphasis mine.
11 John Rawls, *Lectures on the History of Moral Philosophy* (Cambridge, Mass.:
   Harvard University Press, 2000), pp.253–72.
12 Kant, *Critique of Practical Reason*, p.161.
13 Rawls, op.cit. p.257.
14 Rawls, op.cit. p.267. See also, p.261: '. . . Kant says that the moral law can
   be given no deduction, that is, no justification of its objective and universal
   validity; instead, it rests on the fact of reason. He says further that the moral
   law needs no justifying grounds; rather, that law proves not only the
   possibility but also the actuality of freedom in those who recognize and
   acknowledge that law as supremely authoritative (that is, those of whom
   the fact of reason holds). The moral law thus gives objective, although only
   practical, reality to the idea of freedom, and thereby answers the need of
   pure speculative reason, which had to assume the possibility of freedom to
   be consistent with itself. That the moral law does this is sufficient
   authentication, or credential, as Kant says, for that law. This credential
   takes the place of all those vain attempts to justify it by theoretical reason,
   whether speculative or empirical'.
15 Kant, *Critique of Practical Reason*, p.3.
16 Jürgen Habermas, *Knowledge and Human Interests* (Cambridge: Polity,
   1987), p.380, emphasis mine.

17 See Onora O'Neill, *Towards Justice and Virtue* (Cambridge: Cambridge University Press, 1996), p.5–6.

18 Christine Korsgaard, *The Sources of Normativity* (Cambridge: Cambridge University Press, 1996).

19 Thanks to a conversation with Michael Morgan, after this chapter was drafted I came across David G. Sussman's *The Idea of Humanity. Anthropology and Anthroponomy in Kant's Ethics* (New York and London: Routledge, 2001). This book contains a fascinating and extended discussion of the importance of the fact of reason in Kant's ethics and which is consonant with much that I say above. Of particular interest is Sussman's insistence that the auto-authentification or circularity of Kant's argument for the fact of reason is not vicious and does not serve as a breeding ground for moral scepticism, but reveals something essential about moral experience (see 'Morality and its Circle', ibid. pp.21–69).

20 Rawls, op.cit. p.302.

21 Kant, *The Moral Law*, trans. H.J. Paton (London: Hutchinson, 1948 [1785]), p.121.

22 Fichte, *Introductions to the Wissenschaftslehre*, trans. and ed. D. Breazeale (Indianapolis: Hackett, 1994), p.46.

23 Ibid., p.50.

24 Ibid., p.56.

25 Quoted in Henrich, op.cit. p.69.

26 This is not, of course, the whole story and there is an interesting literature on the question of intersubjectivity in Fichte and, in particular, the question of the summons or *Aufforderung* of the other person in the 1796 *Naturrechtsabhandlung*. On this issue, see Axel Honneth, 'Die transzendentale Notwendigkeit von Intersubjektivität (Zweiter Lehrsatz: § 3)' in Jean-Christophe Merle (ed.), *Fichte: Grundlage des Naturrechts. Ein kooperativer Kommentar* (Berlin: Akademie-Verlag, 2001) pp.63–80.

27 Pinkard, *Hegel's Phenomenology: The Sociality of Reason* (Cambridge: Cambridge University Press, 1994).

28 Karl Marx, *Early Political Writings*, ed. J. O'Malley (Cambridge: Cambridge University Press, 1994), p.118.

29 See Etienne Balibar's analysis of Marx in *The Philosophy of Marx*, trans. Chris Turner (London and New York: Verso, 1995), p.21. See also Peter Osborne's luminous presentation of Marx's materialism of practice in *How to Read Marx* (London: Granta, 2005).

30 Martin Heidegger, *Being and Time*, trans. J. Macquarrie and E. Robinson (Oxford: Blackwell, 1962), p.275; emphasis in the original.

31 I recognize that this is a hugely tendentious and partial reading of conscience in *Being and Time*, which must, at the very least, be rendered more nuanced. I have begun this task in 'Enigma Variations – An Interpretation of Heidegger's *Sein und Zeit*' in *Ratio*, Vol.XV, No.2 (2002), pp.154–75, and will continue it in a future book.

32 A related probing of the theme of autonomy can be found in the recent work of Stephen White where he argues that autonomy might well be necessary in any ethics, but on its own it is not sufficient to give expression to the experiences of affect, dependency, connectedness and finitude that might begin to address the problem of motivation in moral and political life. See his 'Weak Ontology: Genealogy and Critical Issues', *The Hedgehog Review*, Vol.7, No.2 (Summer 2005), pp.11–25.
33 Kant, *The Moral Law*, p.123.

2 Dividualism

1 See Jean-François Lyotard, *Heidegger and 'the Jews'*, trans. A. Michel and M.S. Roberts (Minneapolis: University of Minnesota Press, 1990). Jay Bernstein has written convincingly on Lyotard in this connection in ' "After Auschwitz": Grammar, Ethics, Trauma', forthcoming.
2 See Michel Foucault, *The Uses of Pleasure* (New York: Vintage, 1990), and *The Care of the Self* (New York: Vintage, 1988).
3 For a persuasive reading of Foucault's ethics on this point, see Johanna Oksala, *Freedom in the Philosophy of Michel Foucault* (Cambridge: Cambridge University Press, 2005).
4 Sabina Lovibond, *Ethical Formation* (Cambridge, Mass.: Harvard University Press, 2002).
5 Alain Badiou, *L'éthique. Essai sur la conscience du Mal* (Paris: Hatier, 1993). *Ethics. An Essay on the Understanding of Evil*, translated and introduced by P. Hallward with additional material (London and New York: Verso, 2001).
6 Geuss's review appeared in *The European Journal of Philosophy*, Vol.9, Issue 3 (December 2001), pp.387–91. The above quotation is on p.389. Astonishingly and pleasingly, Geuss also says that Badiou's book is, 'by far the most interesting work of philosophy I have read in the past decade or two'.
7 Badiou, *Ethics*, p.42
8 Ibid., p.16.
9 Alain Badiou, *L'Être et l'événement* (Paris: Editions du Seuil, 1988); *Being and Event*, trans. O. Feltham (London and New York: Continuum, 2006). The second volume of *l'Être et l'événement* was published as *Logiques des mondes* (Paris: Seuil, 2006).
10 Ibid., p.9–10. The same thought is expressed in the *Court traité de l'ontologie transitoire* (Paris: Seuil, 1998), p.189.
11 Alain Badiou, *Saint Paul. La fondation de l'universalisme* (Paris: Presses Universitaires de France, 1997).
12 See Slavoj Žižek, *The Fragile Absolute. Or, Why is the Christian Legacy Worth Fighting For* (London and New York: Verso, 2001).

13 On this point, see the anonymously authored 2001 pamphlet from the political organization with whom Badiou has been closely associated since 1985, *Qu'est-ce que l'Organisation politique* (Paris: Le Perroquet, 2001).

14 For details of these criticisms, see my 'Demanding Approval: On the Ethics of Alain Badiou', in *Radical Philosophy*, No.100 (April 2000), pp.3–10.

15 On this point, see Peter Hallward's critique of my interpretation of Badiou in 'Ethics without Others: A Reply to Simon Critchley', *Radical Philosophy*, no.102 (July 2000), pp.27–31. See also Jon Baldwin's and Nick Haeffner's transcription of a somewhat heated debate between myself and a small army of Badiou acolytes, 'Fault Lines: Simon Critchley in Discussion on Alain Badiou', *Polygraph*, no.17 (2005), pp.295–307.

16 On the topic of Judaism in Levinas, see the fascinating essay, originally from 1947 but only republished in 2002, 'Être juif', *Cahiers d'Études Lévinassiennes*, No.1 (2002), pp.99–106.

17 Knud Ejler Løgstrup, *The Ethical Demand*, edited and introduced by Alasdair MacIntyre and Hans Fink (Notre Dame: University of Notre Dame Press, 1997).

18 Ibid., p.28.

19 See, for example, *The Ethical Demand*, Chapter 1, 'The Fact which is the Source of the Silent Demand', pp.8–28.

20 Op.cit., pp.213–14.

21 Op.cit., p.xxxviii

22 In Samuel Beckett, *Nohow On* (London: Calder, 1992), p.101.

23 See 'Philosophy and the Idea of Infinity', in Emmanuel Levinas, *Collected Philosophical Papers* (Dordrecht: Nijhoff, 1987), p.54.

24 'Transcendence and Height', in *Emmanuel Levinas: Basic Philosophical Writings*, eds. A. Peperzak, S. Critchley and R. Bernasconi (Bloomington: Indiana University Press, 1996), p.19.

25 See Hilary Putnam, 'Levinas and Judaism' in *The Cambridge Companion to Levinas*, eds. S. Critchley and R. Bernasconi (Cambridge: Cambridge University Press, 2002), p.42.

26 Levinas, *Collected Philosophical Papers*, p.54, and *Totality and Infinity*, trans. A. Lingis (Pittsburgh: Duquesne University Press, 1969), p.50.

27 Levinas, *Totality and Infinity*, p.291.

28 Levinas, *Basic Philosophical Writings*, p.142.

29 Levinas, *Basic Philosophical Writings*, p.17 and p.94.

30 For a useful collection of essays on this topic, see S. Harasym, ed., *Levinas and Lacan: The Missed Encounter* (Albany: SUNY Press, 1998). See also David Ross Freyer's impressive book-length discussion of the relation between Lacan and Levinas which takes interesting issue with my interpretation, *The Intervention of the Other: Ethical Subjectivity in Levinas and Lacan* (The Other Press, New York, 2004).

31 Jacques Lacan, *The Ethics of Psychoanalysis*, ed. J.A. Miller, trans. D. Potter (Routledge, London and New York, 1992).

32 Ibid., p.20.

33 Ibid., p.71.

34 Martin Heidegger, *What is a Thing?* trans. W.B. Barton and V. Deutsch (Chicago: Henry Regnery, 1967).

35 Lacan, *The Ethics of Psychoanalysis*, p.101.

36 Ibid., p.52.

37 Ibid., p.71.

38 Stanley Cavell, *The Claim of Reason* (New York and Oxford: Oxford University Press, 1979), p.89.

39 Lacan, *The Ethics of Psychoanalysis*, p.52.

40 Judith Butler has recently suggested this criticism in a fascinating reading of Levinas in *Precarious Life* (London and New York: Verso, 2004), p.140.

41 This criticism was suggested to me in discussion with Axel Honneth.

3   The problem of sublimation

1 See Friedrich Nietzsche, *On the Genealogy of Morals*, trans. W. Kaufmann (New York: Vintage, 1967), especially the Second Essay, paras.16–25. Gabriela Basterra produced an extended and extremely thoughtful response to the argument of this chapter that was one of the springs for clarifying my thoughts. For her own thoughts on tragedy, see *Seductions of Fate: Tragic Subjectivity, Ethics, Politics* (Basingstoke: Palgrave Macmillan, 2004).

2 Alasdair MacIntyre, *After Virtue: A Study in Moral Theory* (London: Duckworth, 1981).

3 Lacan, 'Homage fait à Marguerite Duras, du *ravissement de Lol V. Stein*', in *Autres Écrits* (Paris: Editions du Seuil, 2001), p.195. I'd like to thank Jean-Michel Rabaté for bringing this text to my attention.

4 J. Laplanche and J.B. Pontalis, *The Language of Psychoanalysis*, (London: Karnac, 1988), p.433

5 Hans Loewald, *Sublimation: Inquiries into Theoretical Psychoanalysis* (New Haven and London: Yale University Press, 1988).

6 'On Narcissism: An Introduction', in Sigmund Freud, *On Metapsychology: The Theory of Psychoanalysis*, ed. A. Richards (London: Penguin, 1984), p.88.

7 Lacan, *The Ethics of Psychoanalysis*, p.303.

8 Ibid., p.112.

9 Nietzsche, *The Birth of Tragedy*, trans. W. Kaufmann (New York: Vintage, 1967), p.42.

10 Peter Szondi, *An Essay on the Tragic*, trans. P. Fleming (Stanford: Stanford University Press, 2002).

11 F.W.J. Schelling, *Philosophy of Art*, trans. D.W. Stott (Minneapolis: University of Minnesota Press, 1989), p.251.

12 On the basis of a reading of Sophocles, Gabriela Basterra has objected to this reading of tragedy by claiming that the tragic hero is precisely not a hero, but a sort of moral coward. To which I respond by conceding that this might well be the case but that my concern here is not with tragedy as such, but with the *philosophy* of the tragic after Kant.

13 In this regard, see Cecilia Sjöholm's hugely insightful, *The Antigone Complex: Ethics and the Invention of Feminine Desire* (Stanford: Stanford University Press, 2004).

14 Judith Butler, *Antigone's Claim: Kinship Between Life and Death* (New York: Columbia University Press, 2000).

15 Martin Heidegger, *Introduction to Metaphysics*, trans. R. Manheim (New Haven: Yale University Press, 1959), p.151.

16 Lacan, *The Ethics of Psychoanalysis*, p.313.

17 Slavoj Žižek, *On Belief* (London and New York: Routledge, 2001), p.29. See also Žižek's discussion of this position in *Did Someone Say Totalitarianism?* (London: Verso, 2002), pp.82–3 & pp.156–62.

18 See my 'Enigma Variations – An Interpretation of Heidegger's *Sein und Zeit*', in *Ratio*, Vol.XV, No.2 (2002), pp.154–75.

19 See Charles Taylor, *The Ethics of Authenticity* (Cambridge Mass.: Harvard University Press, 1992); and Charles Guignon, *On Being Authentic* (London and New York: Routledge, 2004).

20 The following few pages borrow heavily from the final chapter of my *On Humour* (London and New York: Routledge, 2002).

21 'Humour', in Sigmund Freud, *Art and Literature*, ed. A Dickson (London: Penguin, 1985), pp.426–33.

22 Ibid., p.427.

23 Ibid., pp.432–33.

24 See Freud, 'Mourning and Melancholia', in *On Metapsychology*, pp.251–68.

25 Ibid., p.262

26 Freud, 'Instincts and their Vicissitudes', in *On Metapsychology*, pp.113–38.

27 Freud, 'Humour', p.431.

28 Samuel Beckett, *Watt* (New York: Grove Press, 1959), p.48.

29 Freud, 'Humour', p.433.

30 In Loewald, *Papers on Psychoanalysis* (New Haven: Yale University Press, 1990), pp.43–52.

31 On these topics, see also, Loewald's hugely interesting 'Internalization, Separation, Mourning, and the Super-Ego', in *Papers on Psychoanalysis*, pp.257–76.

32 See 'Autobiographische Einführung' and 'Der Mensch als Lebewesen'

from Helmuth Plessner, *Mit anderen Augen. Aspekte einer philosophische Anthropologie* (Stuttgart: Reclam, 1982).

4   Anarchic metapolitics

1 Having explained what I am going to do in this chapter, let me also explain what I am *not* going to do. I am not going to be able to provide a sociologically exhaustive account of the motivations behind the formation of collective political agency. To do so, it would be necessary to supplement the empirical examples in this chapter with a more far-reaching account of the lived conditions of social actors. What is required, then, is a more sociologically rich and, indeed, materialistic conception of the formation of collective agency and the formation of democratic movements and how specific acts of resistance arise. In short, I am not going to be able to provide all the necessary 'cognitive mapping' on the question of the formation of collective political agency, of democratic movements and the specific political power relations of the situation in which such subjects find themselves. As such, my approach might appear to be too much of an overly philosophical, quasi-idealist constructivism. This is in part a problem of professional deformation and in part a promise to continue the work I have begun here in the future in a different register.

2 Karl Marx and Friedrich Engels, *Manifesto of the Communist Party* in Marx, *Later Political Writings*, ed. and trans. Terrell Carver (Cambridge: Cambridge University Press, 1996), p.3.

3 Karl Marx, *Capital. Volume 1*, trans. Ben Fowkes (London: Penguin, 1976), p.90.

4 Ibid., p.92.

5 Ibid., p.929.

6 See Mandel's Introduction to Ibid., p.12.

7 We might link this claim to Slavoj Žižek's discussion of Marx's enigmatic words, 'the limit of capital is capital itself', in *The Sublime Object of Ideology* (London and New York: Verso, 1989), pp.51–3. Žižek claims that what is distinctive about capitalism is that it is capable of transforming its own limit and permanently revolutionizing itself. In Žižek's Lacanian terminology, there is a surplus of enjoyment in capitalism that Marx failed to acknowledge adequately.

8 In Marx, *Later Political Writings*, pp.159–60.

9 On this topic, see the Appendix to this book, 'Crypto-Schmittianism – the Logic of the Political in Bush's America'. For the wider social and political picture in the USA, see Thomas Frank's *What's the Matter with*

Kansas? How Conservatives Won the Heart of America (New York: Metropolitan Books, 2004).

10 For this distinction, see *Marx-Engels, Werke* , Band 4 (Berlin: Dietz Verlag, 1990), p.475; and Marx. *Later Political Writings*, op.cit. p.13.

11 See *A Gramsci Reader*, ed. David Forgacs (London: Lawrence and Wishart, 1988), pp.211–12.

12 Ernesto Laclau, *New Reflections on the Revolution of Our Time* (London: Verso, 1990), p.55.

13 See Georges Sorel, *Reflections on Violence*, trans. T.E. Hulme and J. Roth (New York: Dover, 2004 [1914]).

14 For a much fuller account of hegemony, see David Howarth, 'Hegemony, Political Subjectivity and Radical Democracy', in *Laclau: A Critical Reader*, eds. Critchley and Marchart (London and New York: Routledge, 2004), pp.256–76.

15 Laclau *New Reflections on the Revolution of Our Time*, p.82.

16 Ibid., p.81.

17 In *Marx-Engels Werke*, Band 1 (Berlin: Dietz, 1988), p.389; and Marx, *Early Political Writings*, ed. J. O'Malley (Cambridge: Cambridge University Press, 1994), p.67.

18 Although this is work that I hope to pursue separately, it is here that politics and poetry begin to collide in a potentially fructive way. If politics consists in the act of nomination whereby a particularity is elevated into a universality, what Badiou calls 'generic humanity', then this is the function of the poetical category of *fiction*. Given the absence of a new political name, we might say that the poetico-political task is the construction of a fiction, what Wallace Stevens called 'the supreme fiction', namely the fiction of the absolute that we *know* to be a fiction and yet in which we believe nonetheless. What is needed politically is a new fiction, a supreme fiction, which is something towards which Stevens only claimed to provide notes. In this way, I would like to imagine the possibility of reading Stevens's poetry politically, which is something I all-too-studiously avoided in *Things Merely Are: Philosophy in the Poetry of Wallace Stevens* (London and New York: Routledge, 2005). In this regard, see Badiou's engagement with the latter in 'Politics: A Non-expressive Dialectics', (London: Urbanomic, 2005).

19 In this connection, see Giorgio Agamben's *Homo Sacer: Sovereign Power and Bare Life*, trans. Daniel Heller-Roazen (Stanford: Stanford University Press, 1998), a book about which in many other regards I have grave philosophical reservations. Agamben writes, 'If refugees (whose number has continued to grow in our century, to the point of including a significant portion of humanity today) represent such a disquieting element in the order of the modern nation-state, this is above all because by breaking the continuity between man and citizen, *nativity* and

nationality, they put the originary fiction of modern sovereignty in crisis' (p.131).

20 Michael Hardt and Antonio Negri, *Empire* (Cambridge Mass.: Harvard University Press, 2000); and *Multitude: War and Democracy in the Age of Empire* (New York: Penguin, 2004).

21 Despite disagreements over the relation of ethics to politics, a strongly allied critique of Hardt and Negri can be found in Chantal Mouffe, *On the Political* (London and New York: Routledge, 2005), pp.107–15.

22 See Stephen White, *Sustaining Affirmation: The Strengths of Weak Ontology in Political Theory* (Princeton: Princeton University Press, 2000). On the question of the relation of ontology and politics, in particular the contrast between a Lacanian ontology of lack, represented by Laclau, and a Deleuzian ontology of abundance, represented by the ever-compelling work of William Connolly, see the essays collected in *Radical Democracy: Politics between abundance and lack*, eds. L. Tonder and L. Thomassen (Manchester and New York: Manchester University Press, 2005).

23 See Courtney Jung, *Democracy and Indigenous Rights: A Preface to Critical Liberalism* (Cambridge and New York: Cambridge University Press, forthcoming).

24 See David Graeber, 'The New Anarchists', *New Left Review* 13 (Jan/Feb 2002), p.63.

25 I am grateful to Oliver Feltham for alerting me to this example. See his 'Singularity Happening in Politics: the Aboriginal Tent Embassy, Canberra, 1972', *Communication and Cognition*, Vol.37, No. 1 & 2 (2004), pp.1–14.

26 Ibid., p.2.

27 Jacques Rancière, 'Who Is the Subject of the Rights of Man?', *The South Atlantic Quarterly*, Volume 103 (Number 2/3), Spring/Summer 2004, pp. 297–310.

28 Ibid., p.304.

29 V.I. Lenin, *State and Revolution*, trans. R. Service (London: Penguin, 1992), p.18.

30 See the closing pages of *Multitude* (pp.354–8), where Hardt and Negri attempt the unlikely gay marriage between Lenin's revolutionary praxis in *State and Revolution* and the institutional methods of James Madison's *Federalist Papers*.

31 I borrow this line of thought from Alain Badiou. For an overview of Badiou's political thought, see *Metapolitics*, trans. J. Barker (London and New York: Verso, 2005) and the anonymous pamphlet, *Qu'est-ce que l'organisation politique?* It should be noted, however, that the views I go on to develop on anarchic meta-politics are somewhat at odds with Badiou, in particular with his critique of the so-called 'anti-globalization movement' ('Interview with Alain Badiou', Radical Politics Group, University of Essex, unpublished typescript 2003).

32 For a fascinating and well-informed chronology and analysis of movements for an alternative globalization, see Simon Tormey's *Anti-Capitalism* (Oxford: One World, 2004).

33 See the Appendix to this book, 'Crypto-Schmittianism'.

34 'Critique of Hegel's Doctrine of the State', in Karl Marx, *Early Writings*, ed. Lucio Colletti (London: Penguin, 1975), p.89. For the phrase 'true democracy', see *Marx-Engels Werke*, Band 1, p.232.

35 Marx, *Early Writings*, p.63.

36 Ibid., p.77–8

37 Ibid., p.83.

38 Ibid., p.86; *Marx-Engels Werke*, Band 1, p.230.

39 Hegel, *Philosophy of Right*, trans. T.M. Knox (Oxford: Oxford University Press, 1967), p.182–3; *Grundlinien der Philosophie des Rechts* (Frankfurt a.M.: Suhrkamp, 1970), p.446–47.

40 Ibid., p.200; p.477.

41 Marx, *Early Writings*, p.188; *Marx-Engels Werke*, Band 1, p.324.

42 Marx, *Early Writings*, p.85.

43 Miguel Abensour, *La démocratie contre l'État. Marx et le moment machiavélien* (Paris: Presses Universitaires de France, 1997). J.G.A. Pocock , *The Machiavellian Moment: Florentine Political Thought and the Atlantic Republican Tradition* (Princeton: Princeton University Press, 1975).

44 See the extracts from *The German Ideology* in Marx, *Early Political Writings*, p.174

45 Marx, *Capital*, p.171; *Marx-Engels Werke*, Band 23, p.92.

46 'From nature I come to *human activity* (*Menschenwerk*). Putting the idea of humanity first – I want to show that there is no idea of the *State* because the state is something *mechanical*, just as little as there is an idea of a *machine*. Only that which is an object of *freedom* is called an *Idea*. We must, then, also go beyond the state! – For every state must treat free people as a piece of machinery; and it should not do this; thus it must come to an end.' 'The so-called "Oldest System-Programme of German Idealism" (1796)', trans. A. Bowie, included as appendix in S. Critchley, *Continental Philosophy* (Oxford: Oxford University Press, 2001), p.129–30.

47 Judith Butler, *Precarious Life* (London: Verso, 2004), p.23. This impressive group of essays, in particular the eponymous final chapter, represents a fascinating engagement with Levinas's work, that comes close to some of the positions argued for in this book. For example, Butler writes of the structure of ethical address in the following terms: 'What binds us morally has to do with how we are addressed by others in ways that we cannot avert or avoid; this impingement by the other's address constitutes us first and foremost against our will or, perhaps more appropriately, prior to the formation of our will. . . . Indeed, this conception of what is morally binding is not one that I give myself; it

does not proceed from my autonomy or my reflexivity. It comes to me from elsewhere, unbidden, unexpected, and unplanned.' (p.130)

48 Ibid., p.22.

49 Miguel Abensour, 'An-archy Between Meta-politics and Politics', *Parallax*, No.24 (July–September 2002), pp.5–18.

50 Levinas, *Otherwise than Being or Beyond Essence*, trans. A. Lingis (The Hague: Nijhoff, 1981), pp.99–129; see esp. pp.99–102.

51 On the tendenciousness of this reading of Heidegger, see above Chapter 1, fn.31.

52 Levinas, *Otherwise than Being*, p.101.

53 Ibid.

54 Ibid., p.194; translation modified.

55 Carl Schmitt, *The Concept of the Political*, trans. G. Schwab (Chicago: University of Chicago Press, 1996), p.28.

56 It shouldn't be forgotten, however, that Levinas's conception of politics is also scarred by several deep and troubling problems that I have tried to identify and criticize in 'Five problems in Levinas's view of politics and the sketch of a solution to them', *Political Theory*, Volume 32, No.2 (April 2004). See also, Howard Caygill's *Levinas and the Political* (London and New York: Routledge, 2002).

57 David Graeber, 'The New Anarchists', *New Left Review*, 13 (Jan–Feb 2002), pp.66–7.

58 On this topic, see Jacques Derrida, 'Performative Powerlessness – A Response to Simon Critchley', *The Derrida–Habermas Reader* (Edinburgh: University of Edinburgh Press, 2006), pp.111–14.

59 David Graeber, *Fragments of an Anarchist Anthropology* (Chicago: Prickly Paradigm Press, 2004), p.6.

60 Tormey, *Anti-Capitalism*, p.120.

61 For the classic statement of this position, see Herbert Marcuse, *An Essay on Liberation* (Boston: Beacon Press, 1969).

62 Graeber, *Fragments of an Anarchist Anthropology*, p.84.

63 Graeber, 'The New Anarchists', p.70.

64 John Dewey, 'Creative Democracy: The Task Before Us', www.bloit.edu/~pbk/dewey.hmtl.

65 See Graeber, 'The New Anarchists', p.71; *Fragments of an Anarchist Anthropology*, p.83.

66 See Graeber, 'The New Anarchists', p.71.

67 I have discussed these criticisms with David Graeber and in his defence he speaks about consensus not as a hypothetical state of agreement, but rather as a consensus *process*, which is a concrete technique of decision-making developed over the last couple of decades by anarchists. Graeber also distinguishes between consent and agreement, namely that one does not necessarily have to agree completely with what one consents to, which means that one can either go along with an action on that proviso

or opt for a 'stand-aside' in the case of an action in which one does not wish to be engaged.

68 In this connection, see Ewa Ziarek, *An Ethics of Dissensus* (Stanford: Stanford University Press, 2001).

69 Hannah Arendt, *The Human Condition* (Chicago: University of Chicago Press, 1958); Jacques Rancière, *Disagreement*, trans. J. Rose (Minneapolis: University of Minnesota Press, 1999).

70 Martin Heidegger, 'The Self-Assertion of the German University', trans. K. Harries, *Review of Metaphysics*, 38 (March 1985), p.477

71 See Rancière's stunning short paper, 'Ten Theses on Politics', *Theory and Event*, Vol.5, Issue 3 (2001).

72 Levinas, *Totality and Infinity*, p.294.

73 See Chapters 5 and 6 of Rancière *Disagreement*, 'Democracy or Consensus' and 'Politics in its Nihilistic Age' (pp.95–140).

74 A related line of argument to that proposed here can be found in Sofia Näsström's *The An-Archical State: Logics of Legitimacy in the Social Contract Tradition* (Stockholm: University of Stockholm Press, 2004). This book also advances an anarchical reading of Levinas and argues for the political deployment of that reading, but it also goes significantly further on the question of the state with specific reference to the social contract tradition. In a vigorously anti-Hobbesian spirit, Näsström argues that the rationale for the state does not consist in freeing human beings from the 'anarchy' of the state of nature by regulating our individual and collective desires for self-preservation. On the contrary, it is argued that the state frees people from the anarchical responsivity of the one for the other and all others. In addition, it is argued that the legitimacy of the state no longer resides in consent, but in the act of dissent.

75 See Chantal Mouffe, *On the Political*, p.5 and passim.

Appendix

1 The following is the text of a talk first given at a public debate at the New School for Social Research some days after the U.S. Presidential Elections in November 2004. It was subsequently expanded for several presentations, notably and memorably at the Hayward Gallery, London, at the Pontifícia Universidade Católica in Rio de Janeiro, the University of Toronto and the City Library in Belgrade in 2005 and 2006. In particular, I'd like to thank to thank Anne Stoler and T.J. Clark for their feedback. I have sought to erase neither the polemical character of this text nor the traces of its oral and occasional origin.

2 Carl Schmitt, *The Concept of the Political*, trans. G. Schwab (Chicago and London: University of Chicago Press, 1996).

3 Baruch de Spinoza, *Theological-Political Treatise*, trans. S. Shirley (Indianapolis and Cambridge: Hackett, 1998), pp.1–2.

4 Aeschylus, *Oresteia*, trans. R. Fagles (Harmondsworth: Penguin, 1977), p.262.

5 Thomas Hobbes, *Leviathan*, ed. C.B. Macpherson (Harmondsworth: Penguin, 1968), p.225

6 Ibid., pp.227–8.

7 Jean-Jacques Rousseau, *A Discourse on Inequality*, trans. M. Cranston (Harmondsworth: Penguin, 1984), p.121.

8 The document can be found at www.whitehouse.gov/nsc/nss.html.

9 Jean-Jacques Rousseau, *The Social Contract*, trans. M. Cranston (Harmondsworth: Penguin, 1968), pp.176–87.

10 Ibid., p.182.

11 Ibid., p.184.

12 Robert Bellah, *The Broken Covenant: American Civil Religion in Time of Trial* (Chicago and London: University of Chicago Press, 1992 [Second Edition]).

13 The full text of the speech can be found on www.whitehouse.gov/inaugural/index.html.

14 Natan Sharansky and Ron Dermer, *The Case for Democracy. The Power of Freedom to Overcome Tyranny and Terror,* (New York: Public Affairs, 2004).

15 Bob Woodward, *Plan of Attack* (London: Simon and Schuster, 2004).

16 Schmitt, *The Concept of the Political*, p.79.

17 Ibid., p.54.

18 Fernando Pessoa, 'They spoke to me of people, and of humanity', in *Fernando Pessoa & Co. Selected Poems*, trans. R. Zenith (New York: Grove Press, 1998), p.85.

19 This is why the recent work of Ernesto Laclau is of such interest. See his *On Populist Reason* (London and New York: Verso, 2005).

20 Retort, *Afflicted Powers: Capital and Spectacle in a New Age of War* (London and New York: Verso, 2005).

21 *Notre musique*, dir. Jean-Luc Godard, Fox Lorber Films, 2003.

22 The full text can be found on: flag.blackened.net/revolt/mexico/ezln/2003/marcos/etaJAN.html.

Index